OSPF: A Network Routing Protocol

Phani Raj Tadimety

Apress®

OSPF: A Network Routing Protocol

ISBN-13 (pbk): 978-1-4842-1411-4

ISBN-13 (electronic): 978-1-4842-1410-7

Managing Director: Welmoed Spahr
Acquisitions Editor: Celestin Suresh John
Development Editor: Matthew Moodie
Technical Reviewer: Umesh Hodeghatta Rao
Editorial Board: Steve Anglin, Pramilla Balan, Louise Corrigan, James DeWolf, Jonathan Gennick, Robert Hutchinson, Celestin Suresh John, Michelle Lowman, James Markham, Susan McDermott, Matthew Moodie, Jeffrey Pepper, Douglas Pundick, Ben Renow-Clarke, Gwenan Spearing
Coordinating Editor: Rita Fernando
Copy Editor: Carole Berglie
Compositor: SPi Global
Indexer: SPi Global

Distributed to the book trade worldwide by Springer Science+Business Media New York, 233 Spring Street, 6th Floor, New York, NY 10013. Phone 1-800-SPRINGER, fax (201) 348-4505, e-mail orders-ny@springer-sbm.com, or visit www.springeronline.com. Apress Media, LLC is a California LLC and the sole member (owner) is Springer Science + Business Media Finance Inc (SSBM Finance Inc). SSBM Finance Inc is a Delaware corporation.

For information on translations, please e-mail rights@apress.com, or visit www.apress.com.

Apress and friends of ED books may be purchased in bulk for academic, corporate, or promotional use. eBook versions and licenses are also available for most titles. For more information, reference our Special Bulk Sales–eBook Licensing web page at www.apress.com/bulk-sales.

Any source code or other supplementary material referenced by the author in this text is available to readers at www.apress.com/. For detailed information about how to locate your book's source code, go to www.apress.com/source-code/.

This book is dedicated to the memory of my late brother, Krishna.

Contents at a Glance

Contents

About the Author

Tadimety Phani Raj is an Information Security evangelist with considerable experience in networking. He has a total of 14 years of experience in the IT Industry. His last assignment was at IBM, Bangalore, where he provided functional guidance to WW Global Delivery Centers with regard to IT security, privacy, and compliance.

About the Technical Reviewer

Umesh Hodeghatta Rao is on the faculty at Xavier Institute of Management, Bhubaneswar, specializing in Information Systems. He has more than 20 years of work experience, and has held technical and senior management positions at Wipro Technologies, McAfee, Cisco Systems, and AT&T Bell Laboratories, USA. He has published articles in international journals and given presentations at conferences. He graduated with a master's degree (MSEE) from Oklahoma State University, and is pursuing a PhD at the Indian Institute of Technology, Kharagpur. He is a senior member of the IEEE.

Acknowledgments

My grateful acknowledgment to my parents.

My late mother used to show me hope whenever I needed it the most.

My dad's unflinching support has always permitted me to pick myself up,
over and over again.

Introduction

The ultimate hope and objective of this book is to ignite in the reader some interest in a subject that many others have found enjoyable. Networking (computers), of which the Internet continues to be its most dramatic implementation, was my first stop on a fairly long professional journey. Since then, I've moved on to other areas. But networking continues to be the only technical subject that holds my interest during periods of both elation and despair.

Communication protocols or procedures form the basis of messaging between computing devices. Whether it's the case of a deep space probe being controlled from a ground station by telemetry or a 3G cellphone downloading data from a video server on the Internet, protocols enable such exchanges of information.

Routing ensures the efficient flow of such messages across the transmission medium from the source device to the destination device. It is performed by intermediate intelligent forwarding nodes called routers. The messages could be journeying through empty space, hopping across intermediate probes or space stations; or they could be traveling through a confusing mesh of fiber optic cables, forwarded by network routers.

The efficiency of these operations is determined by the protocol selected for the circumstances. OSPF is one such routing protocol that has proved its mettle in organizational networks. This book provides a foundation for understanding that protocol, starting with a brief introduction to networking. It does not flinch from examining the tougher aspects of OSPF, nor does it let go of the eager beginner's hand in exploring this topic.

A learned person once told me that I would have gained something from a book even if I had absorbed only one paragraph of it. It is my hope that, by offering a light-spirited but introspective approach to this subject, the reader will learn far more than that single paragraph.

I express my heartfelt gratitude to my Coordinating Editor, Rita Fernando, and my Development Editor, Matthew Moodie, for their patience and understanding while providing critical guidance. It must not have been easy, taking the hand of this stubborn first-time writer who has an odd sense of purpose and humor, and helping him to achieve the book you have in front of you now. I also offer special thanks to my copy editor, Carole Berglie, for sportingly and painstakingly correcting my wayward English.

■ **Note** Chapters 10, 16, and 18 cater to the experienced professional. However, they can be easily skipped without causing any disruption in the narrative.

■ ■ ■

CHAPTER 1

Six Degrees of Separation

We should select any person from the 1.5 billion inhabitants of the Earth—anyone, anywhere at all. . . . He bet us that, using no more than five individuals, one of whom is a personal acquaintance, he could contact the select individual using nothing except the network of personal acquaintances. . . . Our friend was absolutely correct: nobody from the group needed more than five links in the chain to reach, just by using the method of your acquaintance, any inhabitant of our planet. . . .

—From the translated short story "Chains" by Frigyes Karinthy (1887–1938), Hungarian author, playwright, poet

This chapter briefly explores the origins of the notion of six degrees of separation and how it got established in popular culture. People and their acquaintances (contacts) are separated by connections, or *hops* (degrees). This chapter will get you thinking about how networks are connected and how they are structured.

Origins

The popular notion that anyone of us is just *six social links*, or *five intermediaries*, away from any other random person living anywhere else in today's modern world can be traced back to the short story "Chains," published in 1929.

Decades later, in 1967, social psychologist Stanley Milgram performed several similar experiments that seemed to confirm this theory about interconnectedness. In one such experiment, a few hundred participants in the American Midwest were asked to deliver a letter to a target in Boston, by first forwarding it to a direct acquaintance whom they each considered to likely be socially closer to the target. The letters that were successfully delivered needed roughly six steps, or six hops, to reach the target. Milgram described the shrinking effects of social networks in a seminal paper "The Small World Problem," published in the magazine *Psychology Today*.

Despite criticism from many quarters about perceived flaws in the experiments and the conclusions drawn from them, the study caught the imagination of researchers in various fields, bringing to the mainstream the study of social networks comprising chains of direct social links.[1] The idea later became part of folklore and public expression in the form of the phrase "six degrees of separation," when it was used in an eponymous play by John Guare in 1990 and soon after in a Hollywood movie of the same name adapted from the play.

---

[1]Such studies naturally ignore pockets of the global population that are isolated and unconnected by any of the popular communication channels—e.g., the Jarawa and Sentinelese tribes of the Andaman Islands (India).

Facebook conducted a social network study in collaboration with the University of Milan in 2011, which covered its entire subscriber base of active users.[2] The researchers examined all 721 million active Facebook users (more than 10 percent of the world's population) and using algorithms, approximated the average number of intermediaries between any two Facebook users to be four—that is, any two users were separated by an average distance of just five hops, or five degrees. The world had shrunk further! (That is, the world interconnected by Facebook!)

■ **Note** The Facebook researchers seemed to have committed a faux pas with regard to their definition and usage of "number of degrees," by adapting that which was mistakenly used by playwright Guare. In common parlance, including that used by Milgram and LinkedIn, the number of degrees is equivalent to the number of hops. It is not equal to the number of intermediaries, which has to be one less than the number of degrees, or hops.[3]

Stereotypes are based on the idea that two heads are bigger than one.

—Anthony Marais, *Delusionism*

Reflections

I haven't yet advanced to using Facebook. Also, my trial membership in LinkedIn started just a couple of months back. Despite my strenuous efforts, which have been carefully disguised to appear indifferent in nature, the number of my direct contacts is still in the low twenties.

The 2011 Facebook study stated that only 10 percent of their sample (all 721 million Facebook users) had fewer than 10 friends. Such use of statistics can be callous—that is, when it labels a person as not conforming to some benchmark, without revealing the prognosis. Okay, so I belong to that 10 percent despite not being a member of the isolated Jarawa tribe living on one of those Andaman Islands. Is that classification some kind of biomarker indicating a predisposition to something grim? Should I warn my neighbors? Should I remove an organ to be rid of it?

Such a dilemma can be stressful, more so at times when it acquires some urgency. Such as when it's obvious that the person on the other end of the phone connection has unsuccessfully tried to look me up on Facebook and is now imagining why I had served time for more than a decade.[4]

References

Backstrom, Lars. "Anatomy of Facebook" Brief of Facebook Study. Facebook Data Science. Available at www.facebook.com/notes/facebook-data-team/anatomy-of-facebook/10150388519243859.

Garton, L., C. Haythornthwaite, and B. Wellman. "Studying Online Social Networks." *Journal of Computer-Mediated Communication* 3, no. 1 (January 1997).

Wellman, Barry. "Computers as Social Networks." *Science* 293 (September 14, 2001): 2031–34.

---

[2]"Four Degrees of Separation," Facebook Study Report, November 2011. http://arxiv.org/abs/1111.4570.
[3]Ibid, p. 2 notes.
[4]"Beware, Tech Abandoners. People Without Facebook Accounts Are 'Suspicious.'" *Forbes,* August 2012.

CHAPTER 2

■ ■ ■

A LinkedIn User's Professional Circles

Every bit of software wants you to be "social." What ever happened to being grumpy and alone in your writer's fugue?

—Doug Green

The number of hops (degrees) separating two contacts in a website such as LinkedIn can be better determined if there is a visual or tabular representation of the network showing how the two acquaintances are connected. This example will help frame our discussion of the OSPF protocol later, giving us a foundation to work from.

Creating a Personal Network

The website LinkedIn maps a subscriber's network of relationships with other users and displays information about the shortest social distance for each such relationship in terms of degrees. A *degree* is a measure of the social (or professional) distance between people. You are one degree from everyone you know, two degrees from everyone they know, and so on. The free subscription feature, which is gratefully used by fiscally challenged persons like myself, provides information about my network that extends up to three or four degrees.

It is easy to determine how LinkedIn maps a person's network in the first place. Let's consider the account of Tadimety Phani Raj (Dreaded Street Name: Phani the Toothpick) who is keen to develop a professional network of partners and clients for his firm Genial Tooth Fix Consultants (see Figure 2-1). The Toothpick receives invitations from many of his erstwhile acquaintances. Never known to allow previous rejections to diminish his spirit for fresh encounters, he benevolently sends invitations to a few others, including those who can't abide him. Some of the invitations sent and received get accepted, and that's how he obtains his first-degree contacts. They are now directly connected to him, and they form his first, or innermost, circle of associates (contacts$^{1st\ degree}$).

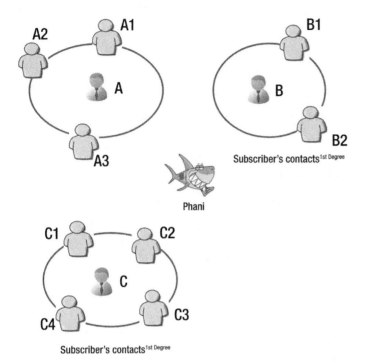

Phani

Figure 2-1. *Phani's (absence of) direct LinkedIn contacts prior to joining LinkedIn*

The direct contacts in Phani's contacts[1st degree] become his second-degree contacts (contacts[2nd degree]). So, you can imagine the first-degree circles of Phani's direct associates (contacts[1st degree]) morphing to form a larger circle concentric to his innermost circle, with the clearly identified connections (links) between members of the two rings remaining in place (see Figure 2-2).

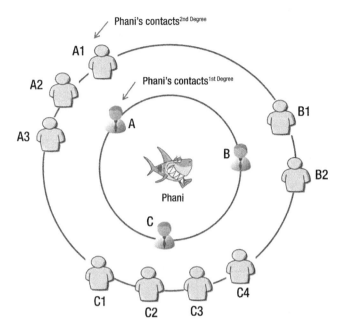

Figure 2-2. *Phani's network of LinkedIn contacts once he is a member of LinkedIn's community*

His network spreads out in the form of concentric circles of contacts (associates). This layout of the Toothpick's network connections, with him positioned at the center, might seem as an indulgent egocentric view, but it actually provides the most suitable way for him to see his position in the LinkedIn network. It reveals the shortest paths to his various LinkedIn contacts and the lengths (number of hops) of those paths spanning the intermediate contacts. Every other LinkedIn member can be considered to benefit from a similar view of the layout, or map, of the network connections, with the member located at the center, or the root.

It is also easy to imagine LinkedIn arranging all the information about the connections of its members in a central database. Let's imagine a tabular view of such a presumable database.

Tabulating a Personal Network

Suppose you have a data table with each row in the table corresponding to a particular subscriber and his contacts[1st degree]. The contacts[1st degree] of that subscriber are entered into the cells when the protocol of acceptance of invitations is completed. Each of the columnar cells in the row corresponds to a distinctly identified contact[1st degree]. This is the Table of Contacts[1st Degree] of All Subscribers, as represented in Table 2-1. Each row of contacts[1st degree] of any subscriber consists of data created and maintained by that subscriber, and no one else. The record of data can be considered as validated because it has been submitted by the concerned subscriber and is substantiated by the identified direct contacts in that subscriber's social network. The data element does not consist of speculative information; hence, it requires no further verification prior to authoritative use in any database operation.

Table 2-1. *Table of Contacts[1st Degree] of All Subscribers*

Contacts[1st Degree] ⟶

	A	B	Phani	C	A1	A2	A3	B1	B2	C1	C2	C3	C4
A			DX		DX	DX	DX						
B			DX					DX	DX				
Phani	DX	DX		DX									
C										DX	DX	DX	DX
A1	DX												
A2	DX												
A3	DX												
B1		DX											
B2		DX											
C1				DX									
C2				DX									
C3				DX									
C4				DX									

DX = Direct Connection

After the Table of Contacts[1st degree] of All Subscribers is constructed, another table is created, derived from that previous table, which lists the contacts[2nd degree] of subscribers in each of their corresponding rows. The Table of Contacts[2nd Degree] of a Subscriber has the contacts[1st degree] of those subscribers listed in Table 2-1. Additional tables are constructed, with each subsequent table consisting of the contacts of an incrementally higher degree. The exercise continues until the last permitted iteration.

■ **Note** Many newly joined subscribers and a few others (as was yours truly) may have no contacts for a while. Such cases are being ignored here. It is assumed that any subscriber is a potential contact (contact[n degrees]) for any other subscriber. In essence, everyone has a network connection, no matter how distant, to the others in the larger LinkedIn community. For any subscriber, the contact[n degrees] equals contact[1 degree] of a contact[n-1 degrees].

Then, a separate table is created for Phani the Toothpick. This table is derived from the earlier tables and lists his contacts[1st degree] in one row, his contacts[2nd degree] in the next row, and so on, either until the nth targeted degree is reached or until all the other subscribers of LinkedIn are included in his table. Table 2-2 corresponds to Phani's egocentric view of the layout of his network connections as pictorially shown in Figure 2-2.

Table 2-2. *Table of Contacts of Phani the Toothpick*

		A	B	C	A1	A2	A3	B1	B2	C1	C2	C3	C4
	Subscribers ⟶												
Phani's Contacts	**Contact[1st Degree]**	DX	DX	DX									
	Contact[2nd Degree]				A	A	A	B	B	C	C	C	C

DX = Direct Connection

In Table 2-2, each occupied cell in an nth row will have the name of a contact of the nth degree. It helps to have a notation in the cell that points to the directly connected contact of (n-1)th degree in the preceding (n-1)th row. That way, it becomes easier to use the table to manually trace the reverse-network path from a cell in the nth row back to the subscriber through each of the intermediate (n-1) contacts.

CHAPTER 3

Router Physiology 101

Technology, i.e., The Science of Trades

—Johann Beckmann, German chemist and economist who coined the word in 1772

Communicating devices send information to each other. This chapter explores the role of routers in facilitating this transfer of information. It gives an overview of network signaling and ends on the note that routers need to exchange messages between themselves for successful forwarding and delivery of messages (cargo) to the end-point communicating devices.

A *router* is a networking device that forwards network packets from one network of interconnected communicating devices to another network. Two networks can be connected only by a router.

A router gathers and maintains information on the whereabouts of all the networks in its domain. This includes networks that are directly connected to it, as well as those indirectly connected to it, the latter being reachable through other intermediate routers. The router's awareness, or overview, of all the networks in its domain gives it the ability to act as a gateway between networks.

The data that needs to be transferred from a source workstation or end system to a destination workstation is divided at the source into smaller segments that are then separately transmitted inside *network packets*. A network packet carries as its cargo a small portion of the total data that needs to be transported between two communicating end devices. That portion which is carried as cargo by a network packet is also popularly called the *data payload*.

The router's job is a demanding one. Despite working in the chilly conditions of a data center, a router doesn't get coffee breaks. It is expected to just continue working unless it is summoned to a meeting to get configured with new instructions or until it has a breakdown.

The Cloud

Considering the critical nature of network communications, it is imperative that routers support transmissions between the networked devices that belong to the persons who are electronically communicating with each other. Those networked devices connect to the intermediate network that is created by the interconnected routers.

The networked devices are typically PCs, laptops, notebooks, various types of servers, data storage devices, and the like. Today they also increasingly include devices like mobile phones, video cameras, and sensors. The connected devices all need to be capable of communicating across routers and other IP networking devices.

The networks of routers are often imagined and shown as a cloud when the details of their operation are not relevant to a discussion. This "cloud" acts as the transporter or intermediary between networked devices, which are connected to that cloud. The networked devices are typically shown as connected at various points to the edge of the cloud. This is a logical representation that serves its descriptive purpose when the minutiae of device connectivity within the cloud are irrelevant.

The networked device that initiates a communication is called the *source* and the recipient is often referred to as the *destination*.

■ **Note** Notice the distinction being maintained between a network*ed* device and a network*ing* device, the latter which is part of an intermediate network (of networks). A *networking device* is responsible for forwarding network packets from one network to another as they journey between networked devices.

Imagine That You Are a Router

While the dedication of a router to its duties is admirable, what makes it truly remarkable is its ability to perform those duties despite its physical handicaps. A router does not have eyes or ears, yet it possesses the uncanny ability to forward packets in the right direction toward the identified destination. How does it do that?

Imagine that you are a router.

You have a brain that is capable of processing data and following instructions. You also have some amount of memory. But you have no eyes to see or ears to hear!

Routers have several physical ports or interfaces (physical sockets) that are used for connecting to other network devices. A few of these ports sometimes are similar to the ones found in the jack panels so common in office cubicles. Employees plug their computers into them using network cords. Each such cord has two pairs of network wires so that data can be both transmitted and received over the same cord.

Imagine also that you have a standard pair of hands. In the absence of sight or speech, those hands are your only means for communication with other routers.

You are a router that is part of a network of hundreds of routers spread across the continents. So you communicate with those other routers. You use each hand to grasp the corresponding hand belonging to your immediate neighbor.

■ **Note** It is obvious that most other routers must have at least two pairs of hands—or more—for continued interconnectivity. Perhaps you have seen the statue of the Celestial Indian, with all those hands, in a museum or have seen a photograph of her.

What sort of communication would be appropriate? Since routers cannot see or hear anything, it has to be some sort of tactile sign language that can be perceived by using only the hands.

Signals and Characters

In any communications, it is critical that each party be able to differentiate the various signals that represent the alphabet or the composite vocabulary of the language being used. (For example, Native Americans who used smoke signals to send messages to compatriots had to space out the puffs of smoke.) But how many different shapes or combinations can even an expert make? Obviously, the larger the number of different shapes or combinations that can be made and discerned to send a message, the larger will be the alphabet or vocabulary of the language, and hence the fewer signals required to communicate that message. But that larger number increases the complexity of signaling and the chances for error.

Imagine that you use one hand that's clasping the hand of a neighbor to send a signal and the other hand to receive a signal from that same neighbor. You are using two active hands to communicate to and fro with your immediate neighbor.

To avoid errors, let's assume that you use only two distinct signals for communication: a shake of the hand (starting from high position to low) and a pull. That way, you and your neighbor are unlikely to confuse one gesture for the other, or any other state. These distinct signals correspond to the *binary signals*, or states of 0 and 1, used in electronic communication. Each of the two binary states represents a unit of information called a *bit*. Despite having just two distinct signals or bits, the router species has developed a code in which each of the letters of the English alphabet, as well as the numerals, is represented by one unique sequence of eight consecutive signals—that is, a combination of shakes and pulls (zeroes and ones). Some sequences are also reserved for special characters, in case you like to use the occasional colorful language.

■ **Note** It's not just routers; most of the IT communications industry follows the same standard, the American Standard Code for Information Interchange (ASCII). ASCII is a character-encoding scheme. Originally, it encoded 128 specified characters into a seven-bit binary. The characters encoded are numbers 0 to 9, lowercase letters a to z, uppercase letters A to Z, basic punctuation symbols, control codes that originated with Teletype machines, and a space. For example, lowercase j would become binary 1101010. Eventually, as it became common to use eight bits (one byte) to store each character in memory, eight-bit relatives of ASCII emerged. These were extensions of ASCII, leaving the original character mapping intact, but adding additional character definitions after the first 128 (i.e., seven-bit) characters.

You might think that communicating in this fashion is too tedious and slow a process, considering that it takes eight consecutive signals made by the hand to just express a character. For instance, how many signals would be required to communicate "DUMB"? In uppercase!? "01000100 01010101 01001101 01000010"! But you need not worry. Speed—or the lack of it—is relative and is just a construct of the mind. Routers transmit thousands of bits per second. So you would be able to transmit "DUMB" thousands of times during the time it takes a human to utter the single word.

- DUMB in ASCII decimal: 68 85 77 66

- DUMB in 8-bit Extended ASCII binary: 01000100 01010101 01001101 01000010

See www.theasciicode.com.ar/ for a complete list of ASCII translation tables.

Vocabulary and Syntax

If truth be told, the characters of the English language are rarely used by routers for communicating among themselves. Routers exchange two types of messages:

- One containing data that is part of the communication occurring between two networked devices. This is the "customer data," or data of the networked devices, that the router is meant to forward as its primary function.

- One containing information that is part of the communication occurring between routers. Such information is needed to assist in performing the routers' primary function (e.g.: address information that informs them of the final destination of a stream of packets).

The data that gets exchanged between networked devices does not get transferred en masse. If that were so, it would be highly inefficient and also prone to failure. For example, if the YouTube video that you wish to share with your friend had to be transferred as is, in a single unbroken stream of digital bits, even a few errors during the transfer could result in an abort and the need to restart the entire operation. Imagine how grating that would be if the transfer were to fail repeatedly, just a few bytes short of completion!

So instead, data that needs to be transferred from one computer or networked device to another is first broken into smaller, more manageable portions. The happy result is that if one of the portions gets lost during transmission, only that portion needs to get retransmitted, instead of the entire file. (There are other benefits of data segmentation for the purpose of transmission.)

Be that as may be, each application typically uses its own vocabulary and syntax.

CHAPTER 4

■ ■ ■

The OSI Model—Division of Labor

Nothing is really work unless you would rather be doing something else.

—J. M. Barrie

This chapter explores how the complex task of networking is made simpler by a standard segmentation of its various constituent activities, as well as by the assignment of these segregated tasks to various distinct, interlinked logical entities for better implementation.

The OSI Reference Standard

The task of networking is vast and complicated. It is but natural to divide this job into sets of smaller subtasks for the sake of simplicity. The International Organization for Standardization (IOS) sponsored the Open System Interconnect (OSI) Reference Standard, which envisioned that the task of network communication could be divided into seven distinct groups of functions. These were imagined to be vertically stacked, one on top of the other, like a sandwich or a layer cake. Each group of functions was called a *layer*.

One of the key objectives of layering was to ensure modularity. That is, the architects of the OSI model were keen that each layer be independent enough so that, if need be, any improvements or additions could be made to one layer without affecting the functioning of the other layers.

Subsequent groups developed procedures or routines to implement the defined functions in the same layered manner. Some of those procedures also become standardized, almost synonymous with the OSI stack (such as the IP protocol). These standardized procedures to implement the various functions are called *protocols*.

■ **Note**   The fact that ISO thought it fit to standardize these functions testifies to how crucial they are deemed to be. The seven groups of tasks were imagined to be a stack of seven layers. Obviously, someone with cake on his mind was heading the committee at that time!

Many refer to the OSI model as the "OSI protocol stack." That is not an incorrect reference; designers have come up with protocols and their alternatives in every almost layer, making it a virtual dinner spread! But don't confuse software packages with protocols. Software packages are distinct entities that implement protocols!

The other advantage that modularity achieved was interoperability. That is, the product of any company could work with the product of any other company as long as both adhered to the same protocols. This interoperability broke the stranglehold that a few of the entrenched giants in the industry had held and it triggered a wave of innovation.

Layering

Let us imagine the movement of an important political prisoner during medieval times; suppose he's being moved from one castle in the kingdom to another castle. As was the norm in those days, the shackles were secured with seven separate locks. The keys for locking the shackles were held by seven different individuals in the one castle. The corresponding keys for opening the locks were kept by seven different individuals in the other castle. So, one key could not be used to both lock and unlock the shackles; also, the shackles had to be locked in a particular order and opened in its reverse order.

Relocating the prisoner meant starting in his cell at the top of the tower in the first castle, and moving him down each of the seven floors, with the locks of his shackles progressively secured, until he reached the bottom (L1). With the last shackle secured, the prisoner was led out and transported to the other castle. See Figure 4-1.

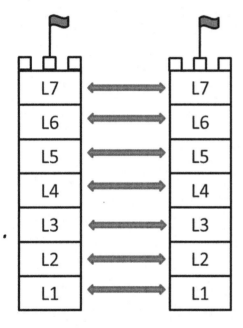

Figure 4-1. *Layering for Segregation onf Tasks*

There, in the bottommost floor of the second castle was the person with the corresponding bottom layer (L1) key who could open the bottommost lock—no one else. After he had done so, the prisoner was led up to the next layer, where again the person with the L2 key waited to open the next lock. The process was continued until all the shackles were removed and the prisoner was in his new cell.

Now, imagine the prisoner to be a small packet of information. The cell in the first castle is the application from which the packet is released. Each of the subsequent seven layers is one of the groups or layers of functions.

PROTOCOLS

It may help to imagine that each of the seven layers has some entity or person to perform the functions of that layer. So, when I state that the layer is performing some functions, as most books do, you can imagine some entity to be doing so on its behalf. When each layer receives the packet from the layer above it, the entity responsible for its functions commences work. These entities also stamp (add) some additional information for the benefit of their corresponding peers at the receiving station for the packet. The heavier packet is then handed to the next layer.

Use of such imagery is not be disingenuous, because you will later learn that the functions or subtasks are performed by protocols.

The packet produced at each layer of the transmitting station gets larger because specific information is added to it; this is called the layer's *protocol data unit* (PDU). For example:

1. L3 in the transmitting station hands over its L3 PDU to L2.

2. L2 then adds its own information to the L3 PDU to create an L2 PDU. It passes the L2 PDU on to L1.

3. L1 transmits an L1 PDU onto the network.

4. The destination station receives an L1 PDU, which is processed by its own L1. That L1 strips away the L1 information and hands over the L2 PDU to L2 above.

5. L2 processes the L2 PDU, strips away the L2 information, and passes on the extracted L3 PDU to L3.

6. The process continues until the original packet of information is delivered to the destination application.

Each layer of the transmitting station adds its information to the packet it receives from the upper layer, while performing its respective functions (without corrupting the contents of the original packet). Thus, information moves down the stack of layers in the transmitting station before it is released onto the network medium.

Each of the corresponding layers in the OSI stack at the receiving station performs the defined set of functions and strips away the information that had been added by its peer, before handing over the shorter payload to the upper layer. Thus, information travels up the stack of layers after it is received from the network.

Figure 4-2 shows the manner of interaction between the layers with regard to the PDUs, as illustrated by the arrows The only PDUs that get exchanged between a lower layer and an upper layer (and vice versa) are the upper-layer PDUs. Consider the case of L4 and L5:

- When the stack is part of a transmitting station, L4 receives an L5 PDU from L5. It then adds its own information to create an L4 PDU and passes it on to L3.

- When the stack is part of a receiving station, L4 receives an L4 PDU from L3. It strips away the L4 information and performs its required functions based on the received information; then it passes on the inner L5 PDU to the upper L5.

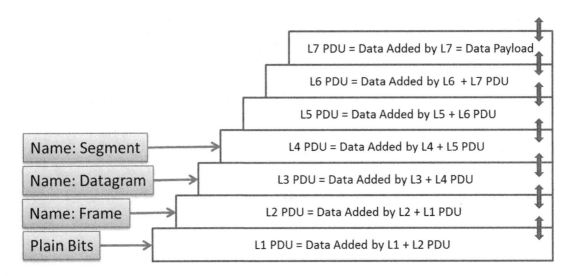

Figure 4-2. *The protocol data unit (PDU) generated by each layer. Notice the different lengths of the PDUs. (Disclaimer: Not to scale!)*

CHAPTER 5

■ ■ ■

The OSI Model—A Closer Look

Rain or shine, snow or sleet, we deliver your mail!

—Mailman's Motto, in the comedy series *Adventures in Odyssey*

This chapter takes a closer look at the standard model created for the segmentation and implementation of the constituent activities of networking. As mentioned in Chapter 4, information needs to be transmitted across the network one small, manageable packet at a time. So each packet may be considered as a passenger that needs to be provided transit services.

Seven groups of functions are performed on the packet in the transmitting station before the packet is released onto the network. The corresponding seven groups of functions with matching objectives are then performed by the destination station, once it receives the packet of information. For example, the presentation layer (L6) of the transmitting station might have encoded the data in a particular format. That same layer in the receiving station would then decode the data to extract the original information.

There are also intermediate networking devices that steer the packet during its journey from the source station to the destination station. These networking devices perform a limited set of those seven functions—only those needed for forwarding packets.

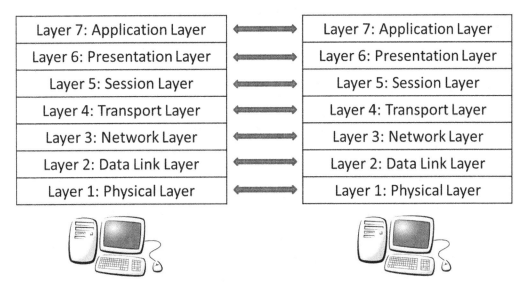

Figure 5-1. *The seven layers of the OSI stacks of the transmitting and the receiving stations*

Let's look now at the seven layers of the OSI model.

The Physical Layer (L1)

This is the bottommost layer. Here's what it does:

- It specifies the physical characteristics of the cables and connectors to be used.

- It specifies the characteristics of the signals to be used for transmitting data over the transmitting medium; for example, it lists the electrical characteristics of the signals or the characteristics of the light signals.

Beyond the basic binary values of 0 and 1, the physical layer does not attribute any significance to those signals.

The Data Link Layer (L2)

In this layer, bits are organized into packets. This layer is responsible for how the packets are transmitted and delivered over the local network. In particular:

- It is responsible for local addressing or local identification of stations. If the local network is Ethernet, every network interface card is given a 48-bit hardware address, called the *media access control* (MAC) address.

- It does basic error detection and error control.

- It enforces a way to ensure that no two or more stations can transmit data on the local network at the same time.

The Network Layer (L3)

This is going to be our favorite layer! It is popularly known as the IP layer. This layer (L3) is responsible for forwarding packets between end stations that are located in different L2 networks (as well as those in the same logical networks!). Note these things about L3:

- Since it is responsible for establishing connectivity between devices that might be connected to different L2 networks, with their own, different L2 addressing schemes, the IP layer establishes a separate, uniform (universal) IP addressing scheme that overrules these schemes, if you will.

- Every IP version 4 device is given a unique 32-bit address. The IP layer uses IP addresses to determine the location of networked devices and to make forwarding decisions. This is called *routing*.

L3 adds the IP address as additional information to the L4 protocol data unit (PDU) that it receives from L4 during transmission of data. Later, any L2 adds its L2 specific address to the L3 PDU while creating the L2 PDU. This should give you an inkling that there are several L2 technologies—and that leads to the idea of modularity, which was covered in Chapter 4.

■ **Note** L3 protocol data units (PDUs) are called IP *datagrams* or IP *packets*. See Figure 5-2.

L3 PDU Header	L3 Data Payload (L4 PDU)

Figure 5-2. The general form of an IP protocol data unit or IP datagram

Different L2 networks might have different local packet formats that support different packet lengths. If the maximum supported length of a data payload of an intermediate L2 is smaller than the size of the incoming datagrams of a particular flow, the L3 of the intermediate, preceding networking device (or gateway) becomes responsible for the following:

- Breaking the data payload of the L3 PDUs it receives from the network (via L2) into smaller units, a process called *fragmentation.*

- Packaging them into separate L3 PDUs with similar headers (a process called *encapsulation*), and then passing the right-sized L3 PDUs back to L2.

■ **Note** The maximum size of a PDU is called its *maximum transmission unit* (MTU).

The upper layer of the transmitting station, which is concerned about losing packets, has no choice but to break its PDU into smaller pieces and then pass those on to the lower layer. Why shouldn't the lower layer be tasked with that activity? Imagine an L3 PDU whose size is slightly greater than the MTU of the underlying L2 network. L2 in the stack then attempts to break the L3 PDU into two parts, with only one part having the L3 added (the PDU header information) and the other one not having it. The net result is one L2 packet with the L3 PDU header information missing. So instead, when L3 realizes that its MTU is greater than that of its lower layer, it proactively breaks the received L4 PDU into two smaller pieces and then adds the crucial L3 information to both of them. It then passes on the right-size L3 PDUs to the lower L2.

■ **Note** The designer of a particular layer will always verify the MTU of the lower layer. If the MTU is smaller, then the designer will need to incorporate the additional services of segmentation and reassembly into that design. But don't be surprised to see duplication of services across layers. Nobody trusts anyone nowadays!

The Transport Layer (L4)

It is at the transport layer that the data of applications gets distinguished from each other—that is, while moving from the bottom layer to the top. The transport layer is responsible for providing end-to-end connection between applications running in the source host and those running in the destination host. The underlying IP layer multiplexes the data—that is, it interleaves the data from different applications that it receives from the transport layer into IP datagrams.

To distinguish the data of one application from another, the transport layer assigns a unique identifier to each packet of data that is received from that application, called its *protocol port number.*

■ **Note** L4 protocol data units (PDUs) are called *segments.*

The transport layer is also responsible for error detection and error recovery. At the source end, after adding all the other values to every L4 PDU that it receives from above, it computes a result using an algorithm. The result, called a *checksum,* is added in the appropriate field (location) in the L4 PDU before it is passed on to the layer below.

At the receiving end, the checksum is then used to verify that the segment arrived at the destination intact—or else it is dropped. L4 may send a request to the source station for a retransmission of the dropped segment.

WHAT IS A CHECKSUM?

Let's say you plan to send a series of messages, over a period of time, to an associate, but you want him to determine that the messages have reached him undamaged and without having been tampered with.

Both of you agree in advance to perform a series of mathematical transposition and arithmetic operations, followed by a summation on the binary representations of the letters of the words of the message that is sent and received (in other words, perform some calculation).

You do that each time you prepare a message, and you add the result at the end of the message and send it across. Your associate receives the message and performs the same calculation and determines the result. He then compares his result with your result, appended in the letter. If the two match, he is assured that the contents of the letter have not been altered.

A checksum is the result of that calculation performed on the contents of the identified fields (locations) in a packet (PDU), using a predetermined algorithm, by the transmitting entity (station or application). It is appended to the packet in a specific place (location or field) in the packet and then transmitted.

The objective of the checksum is to enable error detection, not violations of privacy. The receiving entity performs the same calculation on the same contents and then compares the result with the checksum in the packet.

The transport layer presents two choices of subprotocols:

- Transmission control protocol (TCP)
- User datagram protocol (UDP)

The first, the TCP, was designed to provide reliable, end-to-end, connection-oriented, guaranteed delivery of service, regardless of the nature of the underlying layer. It does so by ensuring that, for every packet transmitted, there is a positive acknowledgment received within a particular time, or else there is a retransmission of that same packet.

■ **Note** The term used to replace so many glowing descriptive terms for L4's particular kind of gold service is *virtual circuit.* The application programs utilizing the services of this layer gain the impression that a dedicated hardware circuit has been set up for them. The service is *connection-oriented* because the packets are delivered in the same order in which they are received.

The L4 of the transmitting station starts a timer whenever it sends a packet. It also maintains a copy of that packet. If it does not receive an acknowledgment of receipt for the packet from the L4 of the destination station before the time expires, it assumes that the packet was lost on the way, and so retransmits the packet.

To ensure in-sequence delivery of packets, and to also avoid delivery of duplicate packets—a problem which may arise because of network delays—each packet is assigned a sequence number, and this number must be part of the positive acknowledgment message sent back. Similarly, if the application is unknown, it could be assigned different dynamic port numbers on the end stations.

Now, imagine the amount of additional information that would be added by L4 to every packet (the L5 PDU) if the TCP (sub)protocol were to be used because of its gold service:

- TCP source protocol number

- TCP destination protocol number

- Segment (packet) sequence number

- Checksum

Wow. We're anticipating what the protocol is likely to be like. That makes us potential protocol designers!

On the other hand, the second (sub)protocol choice, the UDP, is preferred if reliable, end-to-end, guaranteed delivery of service is *not* considered essential. The network application using the transport protocol could be tolerant of some degree of losses, for instance. Or it could have the assurance that the underlying protocols are robust and stable enough to ensure reliable delivery of packets. In many cases, the application itself incorporates the features of sequencing, acknowledgment, retransmission, and so on that are otherwise associated with the gold service of TCP. If the application is just in need of basic transport services, UDP suffices.

Some additional pieces of information that would be added by L4 to every packet (the L5 PDU) if the UDP (sub)protocol were used are:

- UDP source protocol number

- UDP destination protocol number

- Checksum (which it usually is too lazy to calculate because the UDP checksum is optional)

PORTS

If a transmitted application is a well-known application or service, it is typically given a protocol port number within the range of 0 to 1024. Registered applications have port numbers from 1024 through 49151. Unknown applications are assigned a dynamic or private port number from 49152 through 65535, and these numbers are valid only for the duration of the session.

As an example, look up port number 666 (TCP as well as UDP), at www.iana.org/assignments/service-names-port-numbers. It was chosen as the port number for Doom, a popular 3D "first-person shooter" game of the mid-1990s! Because of the cool connotations, this port number also gets chosen for numerous Trojan Horse/backdoor programs.

The Session Layer (L5)

This layer sets up, coordinates, and terminates the conversations. Its services include authentication and reconnection after an interruption. On the Internet, the TCP and UDP provide these services for most applications.

The Presentation Layer (L6)

This layer is usually part of an operating system (OS). It converts incoming and outgoing data from one presentation format to another—for example, from clear text to encrypted text at one end and back to clear text at the other end. It provides freedom from syntax compatibility problems.

The Application Layer (L7)

The name of this layer is a bit confusing because applications like MS Word and MS Excel are not part of this layer. Nevertheless, this layer provides such applications the interface to the network that is necessary for their services. Essentially, the application layer provides services like file transfers, email, and other network services. FTP, Telnet, and HTTP are examples of services that exist entirely in the application layer.

CHAPTER 6

Network Addresses

A name indicates what we seek. An address indicates where it is. A route indicates how we get there.

—Jon Postel, American computer scientist

Messages need addresses if they are to be delivered. This chapter offers a brief overview of the addressing scheme used for networks and network devices.

The IP Address

Every network has a unique address. The address of a network (the network number) is the network prefix common to the IP addresses of all the devices belonging to that network.[1] As a thumb rule, an IP address is assigned to anything in a network that needs to be uniquely identified and that is needed to exchange IP packets with other network entities or to forward/relay the IP packets as a communication intermediary. If the physical port of a device is a distinct participant in the IP network communication, and if it needs to be distinguished even from other ports belonging to the same device, then it needs to be assigned its own IP address.

Note This rule concerning network addresses also applies without exception to virtual devices, virtual ports, and all other imaginable communication abstractions, some surreal.

After the common network prefix, the latter portion of any IP address assigned to an end device is the unique identifier of that end device on that particular network. This latter portion is called the *device identifier*. (The IP address is a concatenation of the network ID/prefix and the device ID.)

Of the 32 bits of an IPv4 address of any device, the initial sequence of bits is the network prefix, and it uniquely represents the location network. The subsequent portion of the address is the device identifier, which uniquely identifies the specific end device within that network.

The 32 binary bits of an IPv4 address are arranged as four blocks of eight bits each—for example, 10101100 00010000 11111110 00000001. To make the 32-bit address a wee bit easier to deal with, each block of eight binary digits is usually converted into its corresponding decimal number. In that case, the above IP address would typically be expressed as 172.16.254.1.

---

[1]For more information, see http://computer.howstuffworks.com/internet/basics/question549.htm.

Note that the expression has four decimal numbers separated by dots; hence, *dotted decimal* is the name for this form of IP address. Each of the four numbers in the address has a possible range of 0 through 255.

The Network Prefix Length

It is the convention to set the device-identifier portion of an IP address to all zeroes while retaining its common network prefix whenever you wish to make reference to that particular network as a whole—that is, its network number. You can derive the address of a network (the network number) from a given IP address if the length of its network prefix, expressed in terms of the number of bits, is known. You let the initial sequence of bits in the IP address for the given length remain unchanged, and then you toggle the remaining 32 bits that form the host identifier to zero. Thus, the *network number* is the *network prefix* followed by all zeroes. (It may help to think of the suffix as consisting of all zeroes, so as to avoid any reference to devices.)

It is also the convention to convey IPv4 addresses (including network numbers) by stating the 32 bits of the IP address in dotted decimal form, followed by the length of the network prefix—that is, its IP address/prefix length. So, if the length of the network prefix for the address used in the previous section is 24 bits, then to communicate the address of the device to another person, as well as the information needed to extract the network number, you can express the IP address as 172.16.254.1/24. Thus, the network number for the above IP address and network prefix length is 172.16.254.0/24 (the last eight bits being set to all zeros).

It is likewise the convention to express the network prefix length in some places, such as in device configurations, as an expansion similar to the IP address. For example, if the length of the IP prefix is 24 bits, it is expressed as 11111111 11111111 11111111 00000000. The sequence of binary 1s has a count equal to the given network prefix length—that is, 24 in this case. The remaining bits are all set to zeros. (Note that no conversion is performed on the decimal number representing the network prefix length—that is, 24—to get a binary form. To understand this, know that the string of binary 1s in this representation has a decimal count of 24; there are 24 1s.)

The blocks can also be expressed in dotted decimal form. In this case, the four blocks become 255.255.255.0. This latter form of expressing information of the network prefix length is called the *network mask*.

■ **Note**   The network mask is not the network number.

A network mask is a bit combination used to describe which portion of an IP address refers to the network or subnet and which part to the host.

—Rita Puzmanova, Routing and Switching

When Addresses are Prefixed or Masked

The network prefix length is a number (decimal form) that is the count of the leading contiguous bits in an IP address (binary expression) that form the network prefix. Either the network prefix length or the network mask is communicated along with a given IP address so that the corresponding network number can be determined in using them.

■ **Note**   This overview of IP addressing refers only to IP version 4. The limited 32-bit length of the IPv4 addresses has resulted in a near global exhaustion of IPv4 addresses. Thus, the global Internet community has undertaken a migration to another version, called IP version 6, that has an increased address length of 128 bits.

Here is a simple, imaginary, impractical, but I hope illuminating example. Let's imagine that your phone number is expressed in dotted decimal form as 153.39.47.55/16. That translates into the binary form as 10011001 00100111 00101111 00110111/16.

Suppose 16 is the length of the country prefix code. The mask for determining the country code is 11111111.11111111.00000000.00000000, or 255.255.0.0. There are two ways to determine the country code from the telephone number. In both cases, the result is 10011001 00100111 00000000 00000000/16, or 153.39.0.0/16.

Now, unless one is a savant, it is better to have a scientific or programmer's calculator so as to translate the decimal numbers into binary numbers, and vice versa. Note: When it comes to masking, you have to work with binary digits, especially when the end of the mask does not fall neatly along a dotted decimal. (That's when you are likely to experience a kind of brain freeze that's peculiar to the networking profession.)

Variable-Length Subnet Masking

Typically, either the first block, or the first two blocks, or the first three blocks represent the network address. That address is denoted by the length of the corresponding network prefix, which could be 8 bits, or 16 bits, or 24 bits. The remaining bits represent the host address.

However, to accommodate the growing size of the Internet (specifically, the growing number of networks), the powers that be introduced a scheme called *variable-length subnet masking* (VLSM), which allows the length of the (sub)network number to be extended, if required, by (virtually) breaching the boundary of the last of whichever of the eight-bit blocks were being used for the (sub)network address. The (sub)network address can now occupy a few of the additional slots that were otherwise earlier held by the host bits. This increases the size of the (sub)network address space at the expense of the host space. Here's an example:

00001010 00001011 10011111 11000000 /26, or 10.11.159.192/ 26

In this example, two host bits have been "stolen" and added to the third (sub)network block so as to extend its range. That change is reflected in the extension of the network prefix length (24 to 26). Note that, for the sake of appearances, the address continues to be expressed in dotted decimal form, with four blocks of eight bits. The conversion from binary to decimal digits, and vice versa, continues as earlier, separately for each of the four blocks. No decimal number is generated that is larger than 255 in any of the blocks.

Let's once again imagine your phone number as expressed in dotted decimal form: 153.39.47.55/12. When translated into binary form, it becomes 10011001 00100111 00101111 00110111/12. Now, 12 is the length of the country prefix code. The country prefix code length has been extended by four bits to accommodate the increase in the number of the world's nations during the past decade. The mask for determining the country code is 11111111 11110000 00000000 00000000, or 255.240.0.0.

There are two ways to determine the country code from your telephone number. In both cases, the result will be 10011001 00100000 00000000 00000000/12, or 153.32.0.0/12.

Remember: as in decimal format, it is okay to ignore the zeros that occur at the beginning of a binary number. But you cannot ignore the zeros that occur after a binary 1 within the binary number. For example, 0010 = 10; 1000 is not equal to 1.

Some might ask if all this trouble is worth it just to set and determine the country code (the network prefix number). Well, you know computers—you've got to lead them by the crook of your little finger.

CHAPTER 7

The Magnificent Internet Protocol

A designer knows he has achieved perfection not when there is nothing left to add, but when there is nothing left to take away.

—Antoine de Saint-Exupéry

The Internet protocol (IP) is the standard that governs activities related to network addressing and the movement of IP datagrams (network packets) between source and destination devices. Every IP datagram is based on a similar format or prototype, with certain mandatory placeholders or fields for information in its header. The information in these fields is necessary for the protocol to perform its various functions.

The information that needs to be transferred from a source workstation or end system to a destination workstation is divided at the source into smaller segments, which are then separately transmitted inside network packets. A network packet carries as cargo a small portion of the total information that needs to be transported between two communicating end devices. That portion which is carried as cargo by a network packet is also popularly called the *data payload*.

The Structure of an IP Datagram

Every network packet (IP datagram) conforms to the same standard format or template. That is, the packet is divided into sections, with each section reserved as the placeholder (field or location) for data of a specific purpose. There is a variable-length field in the network packet that carries the data payload as cargo. The IP addresses of the source and destination workstations or end systems are placed in defined, fixed-length locations (fields) in the standard template of the network packet. The networking devices or routers need to look at the destination address (at a minimum) to perform their routing functions.

Figure 7-1 shows the arrangement of the various fields within the structure of an IP datagram. This figure is meant to be studied from left to right, top to bottom, or to be more illustrative, by moving your head and eyes typewriter style over the material.

Bit	0	3	7	15	19	23	31
0	VERSION	HLEN	SERVICE TYPE	TOTAL LENGTH			
32	IDENTIFICATION			FLAGS	FRAGMENT OFFSET		
64	TIME TO LIVE		PROTOCOL	HEADER CHECKSUM			
96	SOURCE IP ADDRESS						
128	DESTINATION IP ADDRESS						
160	IP OPTIONS (IF ANY)					PADDING	
192	DATA PAYLOAD						
224	DATA PAYLOAD						

Figure 7-1. *Format of an IP datagram*

■ **Note** A variable-length field in a network packet naturally has minimum and maximum permissible limits. But even so, it is a design luxury. Compare this to fixed length fields, where the network simply rejects different sizes instead of trimming them or padding them up.

MOST SIGNIFICANT BIT

In Figure 7-1, the most significant bit (MSB) comes first, to the extreme left, but it is assigned a bit address of 0. I find this a departure from (my) instinct; however, the bits are numbered (addressed) in this fashion. This arrangement has become the convention when interpreting computer words while they are being transmitted in data networks, and it is called *big endianness*.

In big endian, the most significant data element (i.e., the big end) is stored in the smallest address. In little endian, the least significant data element is stored in the smallest address.

Another curiosity worth noting about Figure 7-1 is that the address starts from 0 instead of 1. That's similar to the preference that many Europeans have to refer to the bottommost floor of a building as the ground floor, or floor 0. That's because it is then easier to tell the position of any floor relative to the ground floor, which is the base position.

Suggestion for exploration: Endianness—Why do computers start counting at zero?

The Fields of an IP Datagram

The fields of an IP datagram are as follows:

Version

This is a four-bit field. It specifies the version of IP protocol being used to create the datagram.

Header Length

This is a four-bit field. It gives the datagram header length measured in 32-bit words or units (multiples of 32 bits). All the fields in the header have a fixed length except for the IP Options and Padding fields. The most common header, which contains no options and no padding, measures 160 bits, or 5 × 32 bits. The header length field value is equal to 5.

Differentiated Services

This field (DiffServ) is designed to carry information that provides quality-of-service features, such as prioritized delivery, for marked IP datagrams over others. Service discrimination is realized by mapping the "codepoint" contained in the DiffServ field in the IP packet header to a particular forwarding treatment at each networking device along its path.

Total Length

This, as seen in Figure 7-1, is a 16-bit field. It gives the length of the IP datagram (header + data payload) in octets. Because the Total Length field is 16 bits long, the maximum possible size of an IP datagram is $(2^{16}-1)$, or 65235 octets.

Fragmentation and Reassembly

Chapter 5 mentioned that the intermediate networking devices perform a limited set of the open system interconnect (OSI)'s seven functions: only those needed for forwarding packets. Traditionally, these have been limited to the lower three layers.

This fits in with another declaration made in Chapter 5. If the maximum supported length of the data payload of an intermediate L2 is smaller than the size of the received datagrams, the L3 (IP layer) of the intermediate networking device (gateway) becomes responsible for the following:

- Breaking the data payload of the IP datagrams it receives from the network (via L2) into smaller units (fragmentation).

- Packaging the units into separate IP datagrams with similar headers (encapsulation), and then passing these right-sized datagrams back to L2.

Figure 7-2 might at first appear quite puzzling, because until now we've mostly been talking about direct communication between the source and the destination stations. We cleaned our glasses a bit to see that this required interactions between peer layers of the end stations. So, we would expect intermediate networking devices to perform their function of steering the packets from the source station to the destination station without gate-crashing the party. Wouldn't we?

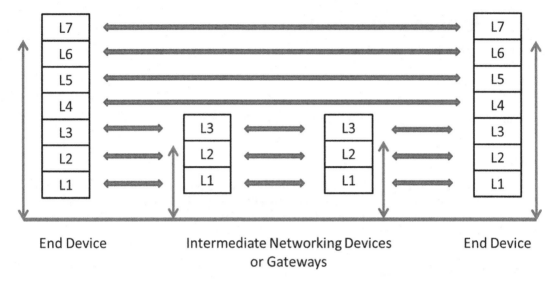

Figure 7-2. *The interactions between various layers across networks, as well as by intermediate networking devices (See also Figure 5-1.)*

Well, that's right. The discreet gentlemen that most networking devices (gateways) are, they don't exactly interfere—they just intercede. A networking euphemism for what they do is "intercept." And this term provides greater clarity to the process.

As long as the interaction between two peer layers on two communicating end stations is unencrypted, it can be intercepted by an intermediate networking device, and the corresponding layer in that networking device's stack can study its (intercepted) PDU information. Those with *mala fide* intentions can make malicious changes to the contents; some may prefer just to eavesdrop. Those intermediate networking devices (gateways) that are authenticated and authorized to perform L3 routing, however, will use the learned information to forward the intercepted packet along the right path to its final destination.

Traditionally, networking devices (gateways) have operated at up to L3. Now we have devices that claim to operate right on up to the top of the stack, but those claims are beyond the scope of this book. In any case, those networking devices do not qualify as high-performance (core) gateways. In sum, I hope this explanation has provided some instinctive understanding of how networking devices intercept packets and perform their IP functions on those packets. Figure 7-2 illustrates that.

The key IP functions performed by networking devices on intercepted packets are as follows:

- *IP routing* (to be discussed in detail in subsequent chapters).

- *Fragmentation* Fragmenting a datagram means segmenting its data payload into smaller pieces and encapsulating those pieces in new IP datagrams (PDUs), which have IP headers with field values that are almost identical to that of the original datagram.

Most of the fields in the header of each fragment have information that is a copy of what is present in the corresponding fields of the header of the original datagram.

The destination station starts a reassembly timer when it receives an initial fragment. If the timer expires before all the remaining fragments arrive, the station discards the batches of fragments it has received, without processing the datagram. Thus, the probability of datagram loss increases when fragmentation happens, because loss of a single fragment can result in loss of an entire datagram. Nevertheless, reassembly of fragments is considered better done at the receiving station rather than by one of the intermediate gateways (even though fragmentation is done by one of them).

Identification

This field has a unique integer that is used for identifying the datagram. When the datagram is fragmented, that same Identification field must be in the headers of the fragments as well. This helps to identify groups of fragments as belonging to the same datagram.

Fragment Offset

This field specifies the offset, or displacement value, of the beginning of the data in the fragment when it is compared to the beginning of the data in the original datagram. To reassemble a datagram, the destination station must obtain all the fragments, starting from the fragment with offset zero and continuing to the fragment with the highest offset. The fragment offset field, thus, tells the receiving station in which order to reassemble the fragments of the datagram.

Flags

This field has three bits. One bit is reserved for future use. A second bit is called the "Do Not Fragment" bit. This bit is set if the application generating the data does not wish fragmentation to occur, for whatever reasons. When a networking device needs to fragment an IP packet with the "Do Not Fragment" bit set, it discards the packet.

The third bit is the "More Fragments" bit. It is set for the fragment with data having the highest offset, or displacement value, from the beginning of the original datagram. The bit tells the receiving station that the data in the fragment is from the end of the original datagram. The receiving station can use the data in the header information of this tail-end fragment to then calculate the total length of the original datagram. And doing that will help it determine if all the fragments have arrived yet.

Time to Live Field

This field specifies how long, in seconds, the datagram is permitted to remain in the network. Since this Time to Live (TTL) field is eight bits long, the maximum TTL is 2^8-1 seconds, or 255 seconds.

Whenever a packet is inserted into the system, its TTL is set to the maximum. Every networking device that subsequently processes the packet is then expected to decrement the TTL field by one second. Additionally, the networking device is expected to keep a record of the time, in seconds, that it takes to process the datagram and decrement the TTL counter accordingly.

Whenever the TTL field reaches zero, the networking device that is processing the datagram drops it and sends an error message back to the source. This ensures that datagrams do not travel around in circles because of routing errors. (We've all faced such situations when we've followed incorrect directions. It's best to go home after a while and leave the challenge of reaching that destination for another day!)

Protocol

This field identifies the higher layer (L4) protocol carried inside the datagram. It is typically either a transport-layer protocol (TCP or UDP) or an encapsulated network-layer protocol (IP in IP, IPsec, etc.).

Header Checksum

This field is 16 bits long. The header checksum is calculated only across the header of the IP datagram, not over the entire packet. At each hop, the networking device receiving the datagram does the same checksum calculation; on a mismatch, it discards the datagram as damaged.

When a packet arrives at a networking device, the device is expected to decrement the TTL field by at least 1. This compels the gateway or networking device to calculate a new checksum for the packet before releasing it into the network!

IP Options and Padding

The variable-length IP Options field is primarily used for network testing or debugging; its use is optional. The Padding field is dependent upon that IP Options field.

EXERCISE

For fun, figure out which fields in the headers of the fragments of a datagram would have contents likely to be different from each other, and different from those in the header of the original datagram.

CHAPTER 8

■ ■ ■

A Router's Got to Learn Its Routing Table ...

It is a well-documented fact that guys will not ask for directions. This is a biological thing. This is why it takes several million sperm cells ... to locate a female egg, despite the fact that the egg is, relative to them, the size of Wisconsin.

—Dave Barry, humorist

Every router needs to eventually build its own information table, which contains the addresses of all the reachable networks in the domain, as well as the address of the next hop router or network directly connected to the router for each of those destination networks. This chapter discusses how routers and their protocols determine the best routes for sending data packets.

Some Reflections on Maps and Directions

As kids, most of us have played some variation on a game that requires us to trace our path through a maze. The problem with a maze, which has paths intersecting at several points along a path, is that we can end up at some location other than our intended one, or even back at the start.

I frequently encounter a similar challenge: the maze of corridors and cubicles in a typical office building. Every floor has a hall, or path, that follows the building's walls and that never seems to end. In between are the workspaces that have been divided into bays and cubicles by means of partitions. Even if the partitions are only head high, I still get lost. For a coffee addict like me, office layouts are byzantine mazes that have to be negotiated so as to reach the coffee machine. It's always my top priority to learn the quickest path to the closest coffee machine. After all, I often need to rush there for a caffeine fix whenever work demands that I stay alert. The journey takes me along a path strewn with unforeseen obstacles—potted plants, mop trolleys, others aimlessly strolling; one is often forced to consider taking an alternate path. As fate would have it, I suffer from a poor sense of direction. Most evenings, I spend some time figuring out where I had parked my vehicle that morning.

Often, there are maps or floor plans on display in these office situations. A person can look at the map to figure out the shortest path to a particular destination. Yet even if the destination were to be the same for different people, the shortest path for each individual is typically different, depending on where that person is currently standing. The floor plan mirrors the arrangement of the entire floor, so the same plan is used by all the individuals.

An individual might mentally change the displayed horizontal or top-down view by positioning himself in the center or at some starting edge of the map; he can then determine where the landmarks are and where the paths lead. Those like me whose imaginations fail in matters of practical utility can be seen slanting their heads at different angles as they force themselves into the map setting.

Networks as Graphs

Graph theory is the study of graphs, or mathematical structures that model object relationships that occur as pairs. A graph consists of vertices (nodes or destinations) and the arcs (edges or links) that connect them. Networks are represented as graphs that show the flow of data, much as that floor plan for an office building shows the pathways for the flow of people.

A network graph is considered to be *directed* when movement over some edges, or arcs, is permitted only in one direction, as is the case with one-way streets. On a graph, the permitted direction along an edge is indicated by an arrow pointing in the right way, just as is done on some street maps.

Contrary to a map or graph that portrays an established floor plan or a concrete street arrangement, you can change the shape of a network graph in a diagrammatic representation by shifting the position of its vertices (nodes)—without fear of causing a traffic pileup. What matters most is which nodes are connected to which others, and by how many links. Depending on the purpose and circumstances, certain attributes associated with the nodes and edges are treated as crucial, while others get disregarded because they're considered trivial or irrelevant.

■ **Note** In this discussion of vertices and edges, I am not suggesting that the geographic coordinates (latitude and longitude) of locations are never relevant. These coordinates are inputs used by applications like the virtual assistants in vehicles. They work with a GPS to calculate distance and determine directions for drivers. Such attributes are computationally treated as additional properties, or variables, that are associated with the edges and vertices in a network; just as distance is a common "cost," or attribute, associated with an edge (path) in a graph.

Here's a gaming perspective on this network tangle:

- There is the graph, or network layout.

- There is the computational system and the users.

- The graph is an abstraction to describe the network in terms of attributes, variables, and relationships.

- The computational system does not pass judgment on how a user's imagination chooses to view the layout while playing the game. It obligingly provides whatever possible information and views the user demands, as long as the relevant characteristics of the graph system (variables, equations, etc.) are not violated.

You may wonder why users would want to have different computational views of the same layout—and why it should matter. Consider the situation of a pilot flying a fighter jet who gets caught in a dogfight and who is anxious about a nasty rear-seeking missile that seems to be overtaking him. We can confidently assume that, given the circumstances, he won't care much for a sepia print of the missile's graceful trajectory or its wispy contrail. All he wants to see on his console in those few, crucial remaining moments is what he'll need for deciding what to do next.

■ **Note** The shortest path from node A to node B could be different from that of from B to A. If any of the intermediate edges is a one-way direction, the destination becomes inaccessible from the opposite direction. That is why the shortest path is traced from the identified start position and moves toward the final destination, instead of the other way around.

No two persons ever read the same book.

—Edmund Wilson, American literary critic

The Attributes of a Route

In considering the transmission of data, we need to account for the possibility that a destination workstation might not be in a network that is directly connected to the source router. If so, then at best the source router can only relay those network packets to a neighboring router, which it is hoped will do the same until there is eventual delivery to the destination. In such a case, each sending router identifies the neighboring router that has been determined (in advance) to be next in the network path toward the destination.

The network packet is thus transmitted through the router's physical port/interface that is connected to the identified neighboring router. So, it is obvious that there are two distinct stages in this procedure. The first is route determination (routing); the second is forwarding the packet through the outgoing interface along the identified route.

There is a remaining challenge in the route determination, however. There is always the possibility that there are several paths to the destination, diverging from that router or intersecting elsewhere downstream. That's why a source router needs to identify *all* the possible routes leading from that router to the destination; only then can it determine the most appropriate path and identify the correct neighboring router.

The criterion for determining the appropriate route is selected in advance, during configuration of the source router. The criterion is also called the *cost* of a route. Open Shortest Path First (OSPF), the routing protocol for IP networks, calculates the cost of a path, or route, as the sum of the costs of the component links that constitute the path. The higher the cost, the lower the preference for choosing that path. For example, the least costly might be the path with the least number of hops.

Determining the cost of a path can utilize any of the following parameters:

- The cost associated with each link, set to unity. That is, the total cost of a route comprises the number of hops between the source router and the destination router.

- Different weights assigned to different links, based on preference. That is, the cost of the route is a summation of the weights of the component links.

- An inverse function of the transmission capacity of the interface connected to the link. That is, the inverse function is used to ensure that a higher performance cost is associated with lower transmission capability.

- Transmission delay across a link.

- Link charges.

- Random choice or gut instinct. "She loves me, She loves me not. . .; this link costs me, she costs me not. . . ."

A route to any destination network is typically referred to in terms of a pair of attributes that make it unique and meaningful from the concerned router's perspective:

- The address of the neighboring router lying next in the path to the destination and/or is the associated outgoing physical interface.

- The cost associated with that path to the given destination.

Keeping these attributes in mind, we can conclude that a source router needs to learn the following information to perform its function of forwarding the network packet from one network to another (including those not directly connected to it):

1. A list of the addresses of networks present in its routing domain. Any of these networks might figure as the destination network for a particular data flow.

2. For each of those reachable network destination addresses, the most appropriate path or route from the source router to the destination network.

The route is expressed in terms of the address of the next hop router and the associated cost of that "most appropriate" path. The database table that is populated with this derived information is called the *routing table*.

The Routing Protocol

A routing protocol traces the available paths to the destination and performs the necessary algorithmic computations, using network topology data that has been collected and communicated between routers.

A routing protocol collects all the activities performed for the discovery and distribution of available network topology data, including changes in network topology whenever they occur (raw data forms the identical "map" common to all). It also includes the algorithmic computations using the gathered data to determine route information for reachable networks (knowledge unique to each router). That knowledge is then used by the routers to perform their packet-forwarding function.

A crucial function performed by a routing protocol is dynamic re-routing in the event of failure or a non-availability of any path in the network. A routing protocol has mechanisms that detect such failures and trigger re-computation of paths so that the routers are updated with alternate routes to circumvent that point of failure. This latter function is one of the key benefits of a routing protocol over manual input of routes.

There are various types, or families, of routing protocols. The differences between routing protocol families lie in the ways they perform these activities, the kind of data that is gathered and distributed, whether the computations are run partially or completely by every router, and so on. Regardless of their different approaches, the final routing information that is generated is similar: a routing table consisting of the "most appropriate" routes.

The Open Shortest Path First (OSPF) routing protocol is the one covered in this book. It is widely used within enterprise (organizational) networks. It belongs to one of the two mainstream categories of routing protocols, called Link-State Routing protocols. The OSPF v2.0 RFC 2328 is the Internet standard that describes protocol OSPF v2.0. It was published in 1998, and is a mere 244 pages in length.

■ **Note**   RFC, or Request for Comment, is a kind of document published by the Internet Engineering Task Force (IETF).

CHAPTER 9

"Hello" Greetings from a Router

Mine's Bond, James Bond.

—Ian Fleming, *Casino Royale*

Routers are social devices. They periodically broadcast a big "Hello" on their interfaces, hoping to receive positive responses. Likewise, they eagerly await similar "Hello" messages that might be broadcasted by neighboring routers.

Hello Message

Their "Hello" message is part of a (sub)protocol in OSPF, the Open Shortest Path First protocol discussed in Chapter 8. This is how a router fulfils its responsibility for dynamic discovery of neighboring router(s) on each of its interfaces. This messaging is the subject of this chapter.

The "Hello" message not only seeks out neighbors, but it also aids the router in verifying any newly discovered neighbor's compatibility for exchanging network topology information. This verification includes checking that both routers support the same values (settings) for certain activity parameters, as well as confirming that bi-directional communication exists between them.

Note   Problems in the connecting medium or any of the connecting interfaces commonly hamper bi-directional communication. For example, a router may successfully send messages from an interface but not receive any messages, or vice versa.

The greeting sent by a router on each of its interfaces includes various elements of information. These elements are arranged within the message template according to a standard format. For example, three of those elements are as follows:

- The time interval between successive transmissions of "Hello" messages by the source router. This is called the *Hello Interval*.

- The maximum time interval that the source router will wait for the arrival of a "Hello" message from a neighboring router. If the message from that neighboring router is not received in the given time, it is assumed that the neighboring router is unavailable on that network for some reason, and hence it is not a reachable neighbor. This parameter is grimly called the *Router Dead Interval*. (That is, it is the interval of silence after which the neighboring router is considered dead.)

- The neighbor list. This is the list of neighboring routers from which the source router received "Hello" messages during its previous Router Dead Interval.

The Hello Interval and Router Dead Interval parameters are verified by neighboring routers. They have default values and can be manually changed by the network administrator. For instance, if one router discovers that a parameter value of a neighboring router is different from its own, that neighbor is not added to the initiating router's neighbor list.

■ **Notes**   Imagine if the connecting interfaces of two neighboring routers had different Hello Intervals and Router Dead Intervals. They could end up in an endlessly repeating cycle of adding and deleting each other's names to their respective neighbor lists. Now, that's an unhealthy relationship!

Apart from sharing an agreement on parameter settings, two neighboring routers also need to establish that their connectivity is bi-directional. Here is an example of the "three-way handshake routine" that needs to be completed for confirmation of bi-directionality:

1. Router A receives a "Hello" message from Router B for the first time and the list of neighbors in the message does not mention Router A. Router A verifies that the parameter settings of Router B in that message correspond to those of its own. Router A then adds Router B to its list of neighbors in its next "Hello" message that it transmits on the same interface on which it had received Router B's initial "Hello" message.

2. Router B handles Router A's "Hello" message similarly. It verifies that the parameter settings in A's "Hello" message match those of its own. Router B then notices its own identifier on the neighbors list in A's "Hello" message. This means that Router A had received B's initial "Hello" message and that Router B successfully received Router A's subsequent "Hello" message. Router B is assured of bi-directionality of its connection with Router A. Router B's next "Hello" message to Router A will include Router A in Router B's own neighbor list.

3. Router A receives Router B's second "Hello" message with the neighbors list showing Router A's identity. Router A now similarly knows that the connection with Router B is bi-directional.

Thus, the confirmation of bi-directional communication comes with the arrival of the second "Hello" message, containing mention of the receiver's name on the neighbors list.

The Neighbor Database

The information discovered about router neighbors is stored in a table called the *neighbor database*. A few elements of that neighbor database are the following:

- The identity and associated information of the local physical interface connecting to the network of the communicating interface of the discovered neighbor. For sake of simplicity, let's assume in this case that the connection is a direct point-to-point link from the local physical interface to the corresponding local physical interface of the neighboring router (see "Some Caveats" below).

- The parameters discovered about the neighbor in the "Hello" message that the initiating router has received from the neighboring router.

- The state of the neighbor, depending on progress in the chain of defined events or stages that occur between the two neighboring routers in establishing their relationship. This state is one of the events in the interface state machine of the router; it is common for it to be shown diagrammatically in a flow chart called the *state transition system diagram.*

Some Caveats

The law that two neighboring routers have their connecting interfaces on a common network is inviolate. (How else could they be neighbors?) However, there are many different kinds of networks, based on network topology.

At this point in the book we assume that the neighboring routers are directly connected to each other. That is, the two communicating interfaces of any two neighboring routers are directly connected to each other over a point-to-point link. (The other possible arrangement is a broadcast-type network like Ethernet or Frame Relay.)

There are conflicting definitions in a few books about when exactly the neighboring routers are said to achieve the stage of *logical adjacency.* Is it when they confirm bi-directional communication or is it after they complete the Link-State Advertisement database synchronization? The situation seems to suggest that two neighboring routers become fully adjacent only after they complete synchronization of their databases. This is confirmed by John Moy, author of the specification, in his book *OSPF-Anatomy of a Routing Protocol.* Moy states (in Section 4.7.1) that "at this point the neighbor is said to be fully adjacent to the router.... At the beginning of the database exchange procedure, the routers are merely adjacent." In summary, these are the major states and events in the interface state transition machine of an OSPF router (a.k.a. phases in the relationship lifecycle of an OSPF router interface and its neighbor).

Perhaps the linking of neighbors is best captured thus:

> *Two Neighboring Routers ... their active (bi-directional) interfaces ... there is Discovery ... then Adjacency ... after much synching ... there is Full Adjacency.*

Those are my lyrics. I'll be tickled if they're performed by the Dixie Chicks. If you're bona fide age 18 or above, in Chapter 14 you can read about "Full Adjacency" between neighboring routers.

CHAPTER 10

■ ■ ■

Hello Again, Neighbor!

Hello from the children of planet Earth.
—Greetings to the Universe in English, message sent aboard Voyager I & II

The first step in exploring one's area of residence is to get to know the immediate neighborhood. OSPF uses its Hello protocol as the way a router discovers and maintains its neighborly relationships across its links. As described in Chapter 9, the router sends "Hello" packets to its neighbors, and in turn receives their response "Hello" packets. This chapter undertakes a deeper study of that Hello protocol.

The OSPF Protocol Header

There are different kinds of OSPF protocol packets, but all of them share a common protocol header. The fields of this common protocol header are as follows.

> **Version Field:** This contains the version of OSPF; in this book, the standard is version 2.

> **Type:** OSPF supports five different kinds of packet types (see Table 10-1).

Table 10-1. *Different Kinds of OSPF Packets*

Type	Description	Protocol Function
1	Hello	Neighbor discovery and maintenance
2	Database description	Summarizes the network topology database, called the Link State database, with Link State Advertisement (LSA) headers
3	Link State request	Request for LSA packets
4	Link State update	Upload/update of LS database
5	Link State acknowledgment	Acknowledgment of receipt of Link State update packets

---

■ **Note**   Link State Advertisements are studied detail in Chapter 16, while messages of types 2 to 5 are examined in Chapter 18.

Packet Length: This is the length of the entire OSPF packet, including the header.

Router ID: This is the ID of the router that is originating the OSPF packet.

Area ID: This is the ID of the area to which the router belongs. The *area* is a logical grouping of routers, all of which share the same network topology database, called the *Link State database*. In other words, the logical network topology of the area is known only to members of the area, not to those outside the area. The router connecting the area to other parts of the network (Autonomous System) shares only a summarized version of the topology of the area with the rest of the greater network. The address of an area is a 32-bit number, written in the familiar dotted-decimal fashion. However, they are not IP addresses, and they may duplicate, without conflict, any IPv4 address.

Checksum: The checksum is calculated over the entire OSPF packet, excluding the authentication field.

Authentication Type and Authentication: This indicates the type of authentication procedure in use. The authentication field for use is dependent upon the chosen authentication procedure.

OSPF AND THE IP LAYER

The OSPF protocol is considered to be part of the IP layer. Like any well-meaning protocol, it generates its own protocol header. All OSPF packets are encapsulated directly within the IP, using IP protocol no. 89 as its protocol identifier.

Note that this is the (routing) traffic that is exchanged between routers as part of their ongoing conversation. This traffic does not contain the data payload that needs to be forwarded from the source workstation to the destination workstation. Traffic that carries the data payload is sometimes referred to as *routed traffic*.

In due course, it will become clear that OSPF traffic rarely traverses more than one router hop. (The encapsulated routing or topology information may traverse the whole network, one hop at a time, encapsulated in a different OSPF packet during each hop.)

The Structure of the "Hello" Message

Figure 10-2 shows the entire "Hello" packet, with both header and body.

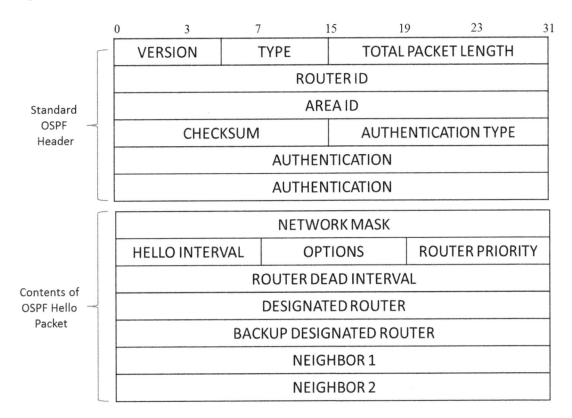

Figure 10-1. *The OSPF "Hello" packet*

The fields specific to the OSPF "Hello" packet are as follows:

Network Mask: This is the network mask associated with the router interface attached to the network. Its presence is interesting here; the receiving interface uses the network mask to determine the network address (subnet address) of the transmitting interface. It then uses this network address to verify that the sending interface is on the same network as the receiving interface.

Hello Interval: This is the time interval between successive transmissions of "Hello" messages sent by the source router.

Options: Only 5 bits have been assigned for use here. The field allows an OPSF router to communicate its ability (or lack of it) to support certain optional capabilities to other routers. The router then uses this additional information at various stages of the protocol implementation to make decisions about the form of relationship that will be built with a neighboring router that has limited or mismatched capabilities. For example, a neighboring router may be rejected when it is discovered during the exchange of "Hello" packets. Or, the router may choose not to forward certain LSAs during the exchange of database description packets.

The various bits in the options field are as follows (these bullets are based on RFC 2328: OSPF, version 2[1]):

- **E-bit**: This bit indicates the router's external routing capability. When OSPF areas are configured as stubs. AS-external LSAs are not distributed to such areas. All routers interfacing to these areas must have the E-bit clear in their "Hello" packets.

- **MC-bit**: This bit describes whether IP multicast datagrams are forwarded by the router.

- **N/P-bit**: This bit ("Do Not Propagate") determines the handling of type 7 LSAs.

- **EA-bit**: This bit determines the router's ability to receive and forward external-attribute LSAs.

- **DC-bit**: This bit specifies the router's handling of demand circuits (e.g., ISDN circuits).

Router Priority: The priority values range between 0 and 255, as selected by the router administrator. These ratings are used in the election of the Designated Router (DR) and Backup Designated Router (BDR).

Router Dead Interval: The number of seconds before a router declares an unresponsive neighbor as unavailable.

Designated Router (DR): This is the Designated Router (DR) identified for this network, as per the current preference of the router originating the OSPF packet. The DR is identified by its IP interface address on the network. (This is to account for the real possibility that its other interfaces may connect to networks where it may not be selected as the D R.) The address is set to 0.0.0.0 if there is no DR.

Backup Designated Router (BDR): This is the identity of the Backup Designated Router for this network, as per the current preference of the router originating the OSPF packet. The BDR is identified here by its IP interface address on the network. (This is to account for the real possibility that its other interfaces may connect to networks where it may not be selected as the BDR.) It is set to 0.0.0.0 if there is no BDR.

■ **Note** A broadcast network is one that supports more than two attached routers and has the capability of sending a single physical message to all the attached routers (broadcasting), if required. An Ethernet is an example of a broadcast network.

■ **Note** The DR and BDR are selected *on all broadcast networks* by the Hello protocol. The purpose of the DR and the BDR, as well as the concept of broadcast networks, will be discussed in a subsequent section in this chapter.

---

[1]http://www.rfc-editor.org/rfc/rfc2328.txt

Neighbors: The router IDs of each router from whom valid "Hello" packets have been received within the previous router dead interval.

The Operation of the Hello Protocol

A router uses the OSPF's Hello protocol to acquire neighbors. The router sends "Hello" packets out of each of its functioning interfaces during every Hello interval to dynamically acquire its neighbors. The IP source address is typically set as the IP address of the sending interface.

On broadcast and point-to-point networks, the router sends its "Hello" packets to the multicast address AllSPFRouters. The destination address is 224.0.0.5.

The "Hello" packet contains information about various operational parameters, such as the Hello interval, the router dead interval, and the router's optional router capabilities. When a router receives a "Hello" packet, it verifies that the area ID, authentication, network address, and all configurable operational parameters have values that match those configured on the receiving interface. If they do not, the packet is dropped and the relationship does not advance.

Whenever a router sends a "Hello" packet, it includes the router IDs of the neighbors from which it has received "Hello" packets. If a sending router receives a "Hello" packet in which its own router ID is listed, it knows that bi-directional communication has been established with that neighbor. Full adjacency may now be attempted.

■ **Note** *Full adjacency* is a relationship formed between neighboring routers for the purpose of exchanging routing (topology) information. Not every pair of neighboring routers becomes fully adjacent.

Router Database Synchronization using Designated Routers

Now that you have a good idea of the nature of the Hello protocol, let's look at the part that the Designated Router (and Backup Designated Router) plays in a multicast network during the operation of that Hello protocol. To begin, let's pretend there is a small group of five friends who love cakes, and so they frequently exchange cake recipes, with the hope of eventually assembling a cookbook. They update each other about their latest mouth-watering discoveries. Figure 10-2 shows the club members and their paths of interaction.

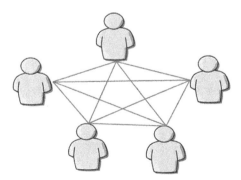

Figure 10-2. *Members of a recipe club updating themselves about a new recipe*

Now, which would be the best way for the members to keep in touch with each other about what they are doing toward the project? Should each person frequently query every other member whether he or she has a new recipe to share? That would require [(n-1)+(n-2)......+1] or [nx(n-1)/2] separate calls to ensure that everyone is fully informed. In this case, a single update inquiry would require 10 calls.

Or, would it be simpler if one person were nominated as the designated recipe collector, so as to speak? Anytime a member develops a new recipe deserving to be included in the cookbook, the in-charge member is informed. That member, in turn, updates the remaining members. A single update then would require just four calls, as shown in Figure 10-3.

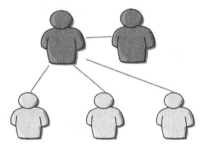

Figure 10-3. *Members of the recipe club get updates from their designated recipe collector*

But what would happen if that designated member were to be unavailable on occasion? Then a backup person should be available. That second person could assume the task of maintaining another up-to-date version of the growing cookbook. This also ensures that the backup recipe collector has communication links with the other members, should the designated member be unavailable. That's the arrangement shown in Figure 10-4.

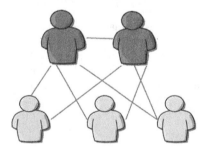

Figure 10-4. *Total number of telephone links if a backup is also nominated*

Clearly, the club's second plan for communications is a better one, and that is why this optimization scheme is also frequently used for keeping databases synchronized among multiple sites. In the case of router databases, the two routers given the task of ensuring synchronization are called the Designated Router (DR) and the Backup Designated Router (BDR), respectively.

Broadcast Networks

In certain kinds of local networks (local area networks, or LANs) like those connected via the Ethernet, the end devices are all attached to the same communication medium or channel, resulting in a shared medium with the potential for media contention (clashes) by the devices. In contrast, a point-to point link is a dedicated (unshared) connection between two systems. On a point-to-point link, there is no contention for the cable medium because it connects only the sender and the receiver, instead of a number of shared devices.

In the case of a shared medium network, the L2 layer, or Data Link protocol, enforces a way to ensure that no two or more stations can transmit data on the local network at the same time. But use of a single shared medium does offer the possibility of sending a single packet (electrical transmission) on the medium that can be sensed by all the nodes (stations) on the shared network. This would be instead of sending multiple copies of the same packet for all the nodes attached to the same medium.

Networks like the Ethernet support *broadcasting* (one packet to all) and *multicasting* (one packet to some), which permits addressing a single packet to all destinations by using a special code in the address field—if and when required. The Designated Router and Backup Designated Router assist in the optimization of router database synchronization in broadcast and multicast networks.

On a point-to-point network, there are just two routers connected to the ends of the transmitting medium. On a broadcast network (like the Ethernet), there are multiple routers connected to the same medium, thereby increasing the number of destination routers in a possible transmission made by any source router. That setup creates the scope for further optimization during database synchronization. Instead of the Designated Router sending its update messages to each of the remaining members of the group, a single message to a group destination ID suffices.

▪ **Note**   Multicasting (one packet to many) is a *selective* form of broadcasting that allows broadcasts to be directed to users who request to see the broadcast, while limiting those broadcasts to only those users who have requested it, thus controlling (suppressing) traffic when applicable.

▪ **Note**   This book limits its discussion to point-to-point networks and broadcast networks with multicast support.

Discovery or Election of DR and BDR

On broadcast networks, the Hello protocol plays a role in the election of the Designated Router and Backup Designated Router. The "Hello" packet contains the router's current choices for DR and BDR. A value of 0.0.0.0 in these fields means that one has not yet been selected. In the case of broadcast networks, however, the confirmation of bi-directional communication is followed by the procedure for discovery or election of the DR and the BDR.

When "Hello" packets are exchanged, if it should be discovered that there is already an active DR and BDR, the new router on the broadcast network accepts them. If there is no BDR, the router with the highest priority becomes the BDR. If more than one router has the same priority, then the router with the highest router ID gets elected as BDR. If there is no DR, then the BDR gets promoted as DR and a new BDR is elected.

However, it should be noted that priority cannot override an active DR or BDR. In most scenarios, the first two eligible routers that initialize on the broadcast network become the DR and BDR. The other routers are relegated to a group known as *DRothers*.

OSPF packets are encapsulated directly within IP packets for transmission. The IP protocol number assigned is 89.

Multicasting for Transmission of OSPF Packets

Some OSPF messages are multicast when they are sent over broadcast networks. Two distinct IP multicast addresses are used[2]:

- **AllSPFRouters**: This multicast address has been assigned the value 224.0.0.5. All routers running OSPF must receive packets sent to this address. "Hello" packets are always sent to this destination. See Figure 10-5.

- **AllDRouters**: This multicast address has been assigned the value 224.0.0.6. Both the Designated Router and the Backup Designated Router must receive packets directed to this address.

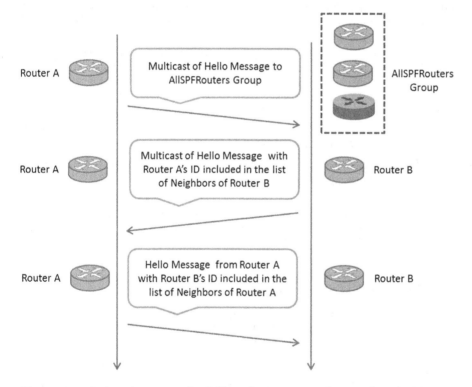

Figure 10-5. *On broadcast networks, Hello packets are sent to the IP multicast address*

---

[2]http://www.rfc-editor.org/rfc/rfc2328.txt

Packets sent to these multicast addresses are not meant to be forwarded; they are meant to travel a single hop only. To ensure that these packets will not travel multiple hops, their IP TTL is set to 1.

Routers that are connected to each other over physical point-to-point links also use the AllSPFRouters multicast address to regularly transmit "Hello" messages to each other. This is for dynamic discovery of any possible change in the IP address on either end of the link. Remember that the OSPF packet has fields for the originating router's ID. See Figure 10-6.

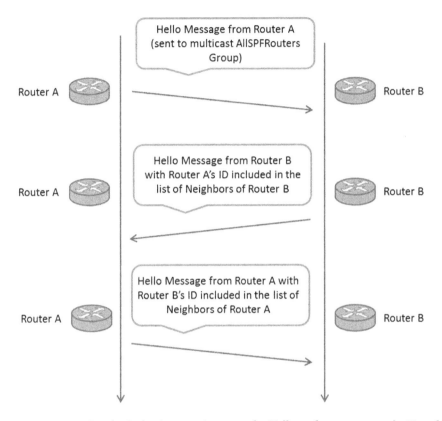

Figure 10-6. *On physical point-to-point networks, Hello packets are sent to the IP multicast address All SPFRouters*

▪ **Note**   It takes a while to get used to the idea of a multicast operation that does not involve automatic packet reforwarding! Obviously the designers of the protocol wanted the receiving router to scrutinize the LSAs in the Link State update packet and reforward only those that needed updating in its database. It's a neat provision, especially for closed, circular networks in which one is eventually led back to the source of the change.

The interface is assigned an address that can be accessed over a network for management-related information. It's a virtual interface, as opposed to a physical interface, which is not used for regular data traffic and is called a loopback interface.

Loopback interfaces are often used in the operation of routing protocols, because they do not go down when the physical interfaces fail.

CHAPTER 11

The Master Table

Cubism was an attack on the perspective that had been known and used for 500 years. It was the first big, big change. It confused people: they said, "Things don't look like that!"

—David Hockney, artist

Every LinkedIn user, similar to a router, has some directly connected contacts. It is presumed that information about each such subscriber is collated to create a central database of directly connected contacts of all subscribers. The record of each LinkedIn subscriber in the central database can be of a standard format.

The information in this database can be manipulated for developing additional databases, one per user that offers a more personalized, user-centric view of the network.

There's One Master Table

Let's review the presumable phases of a network that result in the successful tracing of connections between, say, a LinkedIn subscriber and other users.

- *Acknowledgement of Relationship*: The direct connections between a subscriber and his or her invited users are individually confirmed in the form of "acceptances" by those invited users. When those acceptances arrive in the subscriber's mailbox, the new contacts are added to that subscriber's list of contacts[1st degree].

- *Record of Direct Contacts*: The updated list of the subscriber's contacts[1st degree] forms an important data record associated with that subscriber.

This crucial data record brings to mind images of medieval times, during which legendary kings and nobles gathered to forged their strategic alliances. At those meetings, they would swear allegiance to a cause and ceremoniously endorse each other's skills. Sound familiar? In a way, the legitimate data record that's collected and collated by LinkedIn resembles those medieval events, with subscribers forging a network of contacts and endorsements.

The data record of a subscriber's contacts[1st degree] can be known as a Link(edIn) State Advertisement, or LSA. The name is so chosen because it is a record of a subscriber's current Link(edIn) state of direct connections. Figure 11-1 shows subscriber X's relationships to subscribers A, B, and C.

LSA of Subscriber X	Subscriber A	Subscriber B	Subscriber C
Data record listing his contacts|1st degree	Directly linked to Subscriber X	Directly linked to Subscriber X	Directly linked to Subscriber X

Figure 11-1. *The LSA for a single LinkedIn subscriber*

The LSA is a crucial data record whose logical importance in the scheme of network routing cannot be emphasized strongly enough! (If you're unsure of this, before going any further I suggest you review the previous paragraph, as well as the structure of the data record.)

The Master Database

As mentioned, every subscriber has an LSA that identifies his or her contacts[1st degree]. The LSAs of subscriber contacts are then collated to create a master table, a humongous master database of contacts[1st degree]. Let's call this the Link-State Database. Each row in this database is an LSA that belongs to an individual subscriber.

The conventional way to construct such a database, or table, by hand is to list the subscribers across the top and list the subscribers' LSAs down the side. Then, you identify the cells formed by the intersecting columns, representing the contacts[1st degree]. A typical master table is shown in Table 11-1.

Table 11-1. *A Master Database for LinkedIn Subscribers*

Contacts[1st Degree] ⟶

Subscribers ↓

	A	B	Phani	C	A1	A2	A3	B1	B2	C1	C2	C3	C4
A's LSA			A-Ph		A-A1	A-A2	A-A3						
B's LSA			B-Ph					B-B1	B-B2				
Phani's LSA	Ph-A	Ph-B		Ph-C									
C's LSA			C-Ph							C-C1	C-C2	C-C3	C-C4
A1's LSA	A1-A												
A2's LSA	A2-A												
A3's LSA	A3-A												
B1's LSA		B1-B											
B2's LSA		B2-B											
C1's LSA			C1-C										
C2's LSA			C2-C										
C3's LSA			C3-C										
C4's LSA			C4-C										

Subscriber X = Phani (Ph)

It is useful to leave a little space in each cell for making notes. For example, you might want to indicate in each of the cells the identifier of the row, such as the subscriber to whom the contact[1st degree] is directly connected.

Consider each cell of the table as a unit that stores various pieces of data: (1) the name or identifier of the subscriber who is contact[1st degree]; and (2) the name or identifier of the subscriber to which the contact|1st degree is directly connected.

The benefit of this effort will become apparent when you need to disaggregate the cells in an LSA or when you have to aggregate several LSAs in a row while constructing a specific table. But, let's continue with the subject at hand.

A Subscriber's Personal Routing (Networking) Table

Customarily, the LSA database is then used to determine the contacts[2nd degree] of a particular subscriber. (These are the contacts[1st degree] of the subscriber's contacts[1st degree].) The subscriber's contacts|3rd degree are similarly identified, and so on.

Another table, this time identifying all the contacts of the individual subscriber, can be constructed. Each progressive row in the table lists the subscriber's next level of contacts, with connection paths consisting of the same number of hops, or degrees. This is the Network Connections Table or Personal Routing (Networking) Table, as shown in Table 11-2.

Table 11-2. *Phani's Personal Routing (Networking) Table*

Subscribers →		A	B	C	A1	A2	A3	B1	B2	C1	C2	C3	C4
Contact[1st Degree]		Ph-A	Ph-B	Ph-C									
Contact[2nd Degree]					Ph-A-A1	Ph-A-A2	Ph-A-A3	Ph-B-B1	Ph-B-B2	Ph-C-C1	Ph-C-C2	Ph-C-C3	Ph-C-C4
...													

(Left vertical label: Phani's Contacts)

Every Subscriber Presents a Unique View

The Routing (Networking) Table offers a unique perspective on the subscriber. It helps determine two things:

- The row to which a subscriber's contact belongs will correspond to the degree of separation (hop) between the subscriber and the contact. The nth row lists the subscriber's contacts|n degrees.

- By moving across the rows in an ordered sequence of intermediate contacts, it is possible to trace the path of the connection.

■ **Note** This is an example of an individual table for a single subscriber, which ultimately is part of the larger LinkedIn database. It is not accessible to a subscriber in this fashion, however. Information such as this can be retrieved from the table when a legitimate query is made, such as when an authenticated subscriber's cursor moves over another user's name in a LinkedIn page.

Let us now imagine what changes are effected in a subscriber's Personal Routing (Networking) Table when subscriber Y becomes a contacts[1st degree] of subscriber X.

1. Subscriber Y gets added to subscriber X's LSA (contacts[1st degree]).

2. Subscriber X is added to subscriber Y's LSA.

3. Changes are made in subscriber X's Personal Routing (Networking) Table.

The contacts[1st degree] of subscriber Y now become contacts[2nd degree] of subscriber X (except for those who have existing connections with subscriber X that are two degrees or closer). No change is made in the status of subscriber Y's contact[1st degree] if Y is an existing contact[2nd degree] or contact[1st degree] of subscriber X. It is naturally preferable to retain an existing (shorter) connection between users, rather than create a longer alternate connection by spanning some additional degrees of separation, or hops.

As you can see, changes will ripple down the remaining tiers of contacts, with any contact[n degrees] of one subscriber becoming a contact[(n+1) degree] of a second subscriber. And, of course, there are corresponding changes in other subscribers' Personal Routing (Networking) Tables.

■ **Note**   There're those networking professionals and charlatans alike who prefer to disregard the finer differences between a database and a database table, when discussing all matters concerned with networking. In a show of solidarity with that Brotherhood, I have used the terms interchangeably in this book. It is important to note that all mentioned tables are part of the same central LinkedIn database. No part of the LinkedIn database is stored and maintained independently by a subscriber on their computer.

CHAPTER 12

An Organizational Network

Second star to the right, and straight on till morning.

—Peter Pan, in the play by J. M. Barrie

Today's large and complex global organizations need to link their units electronically, across continents, for quick communications. This chapter introduces an enterprise- or organization-wide area network that could be used by such an organization. The larger "parent" network consists of smaller local area networks (LANs) in different locations, interconnected by routers. To understand the layers of networks and how their naming/address systems function, a hypothetical network is developed in this chapter that will then be the reference network for explaining the concepts presented in subsequent chapters of this book.

An Organization-Wide Network

Figure 12-1 portrays an organizational network that uses routers to link several local area networks (LANs) in different locations around the world. Note that the squares are routers and the circles are LANs connected to those routers.

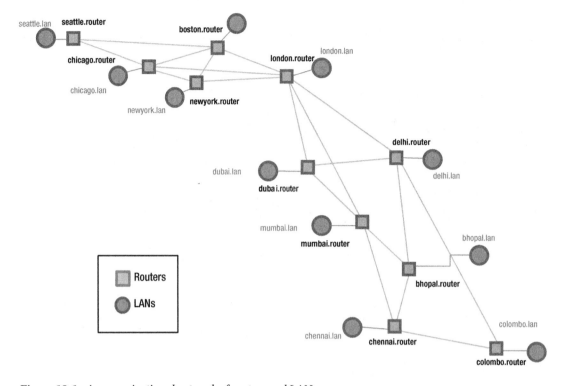

Figure 12-1. *An organizational network of routers and LANs*

■ **Warning** Do not use Figure 12-1 for guidance in a flying test or geography examination!

The Router IP Addresses

So, how does this large organizational network operate? Let's begin with the IP addresses of the routers in our example network. Recall the discussion of IP addresses in Chapter 3.

■ **Note** Just remember that "network address" is parlance for the numerical identifiers given to network devices to greet or identify them. Technically, they are the devices' IP addresses. Here, though, terms like "router address" and "device address" are also used, largely from habit. All that matters for the present discussion is that router network addresses are stylistically fashioned.

Each router's IP address includes the following:

- Elements of the organizational address consisting of two blocks, which are placed at the head. In the example used in this chapter, the organizational address is toothfix.genially.

- The name of the location within the organizational network where the particular router is installed. For example, Figure 12-1 shows routers at 11 locations. The location might, for example, be bhopal (up to 8 letters).

- The word *router*.

■ **Note**   Each of the interfaces of a router has a distinct IP address. Nevertheless, the router itself needs an identifier/address for the sake of other devices and entities. Typically the interface IP address that is greater than those of all the other interfaces is selected as the router's advertised IP address. (If loopback interfaces are configured, then their IP addresses get preference over physical port IP addresses. The loopback interface IP address that is greater than the other loopback interface IP addresses gets selected as the router address.)

The first two blocks/bytes of the 32-bit IP address for the organizational routers are common for all addresses in the network. The IP address in dotted format has four blocks of eight letters—that is, there are four blocks available; each block offers a maximum space for eight letters (numerals/alphabets), as follows:

`00000000.00000000.00000000.00000000/length of the network prefix`

For sake of this discussion, I will use pseudo IP addresses that employ mostly alphabetic letters instead of the binary bits (they are pseudo because they are nonstandard and nonroutable). In this scheme, the total count (number) of alphabets and numerals placed in position within the bounds of the pseudo IP address is 32, similar to the total number of binary bits used in any standard IP address.

So, each zero in the blank address above occupies the available space for one letter (an alphabet or a numeral). The value of the host IP address is determined by the least significant alphabets/numerals. The same principle is extended to the pseudo addressing scheme.

For example, suppose the organizational network address is toothfix.genially.0.0/16. (Just count the letters!) Thus, the first block in our example organizational address is occupied by eight letters—spelling *toothfix* and leaving no space for adding additional letters before the first dot. This is also the case with the second block, which is occupied by the letters *genially*.

■ **Note**   Let's imagine that the ASCII format, which translates alphabets and decimal numbers into binary form, has been replaced by a format of my own making. As a result, all the given sequences of digits and alphabets in each block of the pseudo IP address somehow translate into binary numbers that fit into eight bits. Each block thus complies with the maximum upper limit of 255 (i.e., 11111111 in binary form). (This format has been contrived as a temporary aid so readers need not grapple with regular-looking IP addresses at this stage.)

By the way, in real-world practice it is not uncommon for network engineers to assign user-friendly names to routers for routine use, as well as to their routable network IP addresses. Most commercial routers support services like the Domain Name System (DNS), the hierarchical naming system for computers connected to the Internet or a private network; by translating those user-friendly addresses into numerical IP addresses, DNS makes it possible to have addresses like www.linkedin.com, even though computers and servers do not understand English hostnames.

Getting back to our example, then, the IP address of a router at any location within the organizational network we've shown in Figure 12-1 is as follows:

`toothfix.genially. [the location name].router/24 [the count of network prefix bits or letters]`

Remember, every router in the network supports a directly connected user LAN. So, the network number of the LAN at one of these locations would be as follows:

`toothfix.genially.(location name).lan/27 [i.e., the count of network prefix bits letters]`

Based on this scheme, then, the IP address of a router, if and when installed at, say, Srinagar, would be as follows:

`toothfix.genially.srinagar.router/24`

The IP address of the router at Chennai would then be `toothfix.genially.0chennai.router/24` (with one zero added), but this typically would get expressed as `toothfix.genially.chennai.router/24`. The IP address of the router at Bhopal then adds another zero and would be `toothfix.genially.00bhopal.router/24`. That address also would typically be expressed as `toothfix.genially.bhopal.router/24`.

The router's IP address, by convention, is terminated with a forward slash (/), followed by a number. That number (a decimal) represents the count—that is, the length of the network prefix. (At present, what you need to remember regarding network prefix length is only that it is the second of two elements that determine the identity of a network—the first being the IP address of the device.) So, in summary, the IP address of the router at Bhopal is `toothfix.genially.bhopal.router/24`.

Also, remember that using any identity based on a hierarchical addressing (naming) system depends on the reference or "conversational" context. For example, within our example of the toothfix.genially.0.0/16 organizational network, routers are distinguished among themselves by using a "flat" addressing (naming) hierarchy based on location. Therefore, the routers at Delhi, Mumbai, and Bhopal are `toothfix.genially.delhi.router/24`, `toothfix.genially.mumbai.router./24`, and `toothfix.genially.bhopal.router/24`. However, most routers belonging to another organization would not care. For them, those routers are just `toothfix.genially.0.0/16` routers (with a natural loss of specificity in such an indifferent reference).

The Network Numbers

As mentioned, the address of the Bhopal router just discussed is `toothfix.genially.bhopal.router/24`, with the network prefix as 24. That makes the router's network number be `toothfix.genially.bhopal.0000000/24`. Now, there might be some who are puzzled. We have an organizational network with the network number `toothfix.genially.0.0/16`, with the network prefix length being 16. How does one explain the different network numbers for the same organizational network? The answer is that these numbers identify different networks; that is, one small network is part of a bigger network. It all depends upon one's perspective.

The `toothfix.genially/0.0/16` "parent" organizational network is made up of these smaller networks, or subnetworks (a sub-network is also a network). Hence, the subnetworks have a part of their respective prefixes that is common to all members of that subnetwork—the "parent" enterprise network number. To distinguish one subnetwork from another, the specific subnetwork number is unique at that lower level by adding a few more bits to the common parent network prefix. This results in a longer subnetwork prefix; the subnetwork number for the LAN at Bhopal is, therefore, `toothpick.genially.bhopal.0000000/24`.

The length of the network prefixes need not be restricted to the boundaries of the dotted decimals in the IP address; that is, they need not be only multiples of eight bits.

Any subnetwork created within the Bhopal subnetwork also will have an identifier added to the "parent" network number that extends the prefix further and makes it distinguishable at that level of the hierarchy. For example, the LAN at Bhopal has three more bits added to its parent Bhopal network prefix, resulting in its own network number of `toothfix.genially.bhopal.lan0000/27`.

SUBNETTING

The whole IP addressing scheme is hierarchical in nature and similar to a naming practice supposedly still prevalent in some regions of the world. Names identify common family roots and they trace a hierarchy of related social units. A large community has a common name which is used by its members and that's how outsiders refer to the community. However the community itself is made of smaller clans who have the practice of adding a clan name to their common community title to distinguish each clan from the others within the community. Then there are family names. As one moves closer to locating an individual you end up with some names as long as an arm. Mine is longer, but for different reasons. I'll narrate the tragic story behind that some other time.

Network Devices

What happens when a device is connected to the LAN, which is a subnetwork of that organizational "parent" network? The local network number of that router we've been discussing that's located in Bhopal is, as mentioned above, `toothfix.genially.bhopal.0000000/24`. The network number of its LAN subnetwork is, as also mentioned, `toothfix.genially.bhopal.lan0000/27`. That leaves five bits of available space in the last block/byte of that 32-bit IP address for use as the device's specific identifier (the suffix). For example, the addresses of a few devices in that Bhopal LAN might be `toothfix.genially.bhopal.lansdale` or `toothfix.genially.bhopal.lancar11`.

When user Toothpick arrives and attaches his laptop to the LAN at Bhopal, the Dynamic Host Configuration Protocol (DHCP)/DNS server assigns him the IP address `toothfix.genially.bhopal.lanshark`.

■ **Note**   Remember that, in reality, the IPv4.0 address blocks are decimal numbers (in dotted decimal format). So Phani's laptop IP address is more likely to look something like 10.11.140.261/27.

Network Interactions

You probably noticed in Figure 12-1 that there is only one entry and exit for each LAN or any other possible range of network addresses at those points or locations. In each case, the sole path is through the directly connected router. Such an arrangement is called a *stub network*.

Because the routers in the organizational network all have unique network numbers, as bits added to the "parent" network prefix, they can be distinguished one from another and therefore they can act as gateways between the various subnetworks. Traffic destined for the Internet or a different organizational network is forwarded to a pre-identified router that acts as the default gateway to the outside world.

The hierarchical IP addressing scheme works well because if a router knows a route to a network, that route holds true for its subnetworks as well. If a router is not directly connected to a network (and hence to any of its subnetworks), it need not store redundant routes for its subnetworks. That is, a single route for both the network and its subnetworks may suffice unless alternate routes are more efficient in certain circumstances.

From a routing (packet-forwarding) perspective, the router need use only the single "most appropriate" route listed in its routing table to forward all packets destined for a distant network and its own subnetworks. The burden of maintaining local routes within the destination neighborhood falls on the downstream routers, which are connected directly to the destination network and any of its subnetworks. This approach reduces the size of the routing table (which stores routes) that needs to be maintained by a router and makes it more manageable. It ensures that routing table lookups are faster.

The Operationalized Organizational Network

Let's take a simple look at how the routers of an organizational network operate once everything is up and running. For example, when our router `toothfix.genially.bhopal.router/24` is initialized, it is unaware of its neighboring routers. The "Hello" message it crafts and transmits is likely to have an empty list of neighboring routers, as described in Chapter 9. Let us imagine, though, that all the neighboring routers have matching values for key routing parameters.

As time progresses, `toothfix.genially.bhopal.router/24` receives "Hello" messages from the neighboring routers, in this case `toothfix.genially.chennai.router`, `toothfix.genially.mumbai.router`, and `toothfix.genially.delhi.router`, with itself mentioned as a neighbor in their corresponding neighbor lists. It then completes the three-way handshake by sending "Hello" messages with its own neighbors list containing the three newly identified neighbors. All the involved routers are assumed to belong to a single OSPF area (see Chapter 2) within a single OSPF administrative autonomous system (AS). (Any reference to a routing domain is essentially a reference to an OSPF area.)

CHAPTER 13

The Secret of Routing Powers

You can't handle the truth!

—Jack Nicholson as Col. Jessup, in the movie *A Few Good Men*

Routing is based on the principle that a destination that is n hops away from a router is one hop closer to the router's immediate neighbor; that is, it is just (n-1) hops away from that immediate neighbor. As done in some prior chapters, we look at LinkedIn's social networking setup as a good way to understand the routing possibilities of networks. This chapter surveys some of the similarities between a router network and LinkedIn's implementation of its social networking service. The chapter then proceeds to identify the possible key differences and the implications of those differences for an organization's network.

A Sharing of Information

A router cannot move, and neither can it see. It can only perceive and identify its directly connected neighbors by means of the "Hello" messages it receives through its physical interfaces. So the router's direct awareness and self-gathered knowledge of other routers is restricted to its immediate circle of neighbors, each of which is directly connected to one of its physical ports.

In such a network, how does a router like toothfix.genially.bhopal.router/24, which we identified in Chapter 12, know that a particular distant destination exists, let alone be able to determine which one of its directly connected neighbors is next along the most suitable path to that destination?

There is a magic about how routers develop their routing capabilities. Ironically, that ability comes only through sharing information with others! It's a productive activity that in its various forms comes instinctively to all of us, like those conversations around the water cooler or coffee machine at the office.

The manner in which this sharing of information achieves results becomes evident when you realize this simple fact: a destination router that is a few hops removed from the source router is nevertheless a neighboring router to another router that is one hop closer to the source router. It's the six degrees of separation. It's the way a LinkedIn user who is a few degrees outside your circle of direct contacts is nevertheless the direct contact or contact$^{\text{1st degree}}$ of a user who is one degree closer to you. That is, any subscriber's contact$^{\text{n degrees}}$ = contact$^{\text{1st degree}}$ of a contact$^{\text{(n-1) degrees}}$.

The Similarities to LinkedIn Networking

A quick review of the LinkedIn implementation, as outlined in Chapter 11, leads to the next few steps:

1. Collate the lists of neighboring routers ($\approx$ router[1st degree]) in the network. The resulting table describing the topology of the network is akin to the master LSA database of the LinkedIn implementation.

2. Start with any source router and hop to the next, tracing the concentric circles formed by the reachable routers, as well as the intermediate links that connect them to the source router.

The neighboring routers to a source router form the circle closest to the source and are the destinations[1st degree]. The neighboring routers of those destinations[1st degree] routers are destinations[2nd degree]. If we do this for `toothfix.genially.bhopal.router/24`, continuing outward one hop at a time, we widen the spread of the concentric circles of reachable routers until we get to the last possible iteration. Each destination router is a node on one of those concentric circles. In short, the goal is to use a common topological database ($\approx$ LSA database) to create the equivalent of a Personal Routing (Networking) Table for each router. The final table, in networking parlance, is called the *Routing Database/Table*.

This is admittedly the right plan. However, it's here that the knotty problems of design and performance for a routing protocol emerge. The LinkedIn implementation avoids some of these complications because of its limited objectives, but our goals are bigger.

The Differences from LinkedIn Networking

The LinkedIn database may be viewed as a logically central database, even though it might have a physically distributed architecture—that is, an architecture based on geographically distributed, replicating databases for wider and more efficient geographic reach. But LinkedIn does not have to worry about detecting changes in the social connections of its subscribers. It is the subscriber who knows his or her network status best, and it is the subscriber who is tasked with updating that circle of direct contacts, using manual entry into the central LinkedIn database.

Similarly, subscribers are not exhorted to become database wizards and are not held accountable for the administration and operation of the database. It is the LinkedIn business function that performs those background activities and presents subscribers with their own Personal Routing (Networking) Table, as described in Chapter 11.

However, this convenient division of labor between users and administration is not feasible for the traditional networking world because it impacts the desired autonomy of router function. That is, routers are expected to function effectively and independently, even if a portion of the network in their domain fails or becomes unreachable because of failures in intermediate link or devices. That demand precludes any dependence on a central computing system or routing database, no matter how convenient that may seem.

■ **Note** Folklore has it that one of the design guidelines given by the U.S. Department of Defense's Defense Advanced Research Projects Agency (DARPA) for ARPANET, the predecessor of the present Internet, was that the protocols ensure the network would survive a nuclear attack. Even if some nodes (routers) were to become unavailable because of the blast, the network had to continue to function by automatically rerouting traffic around the points of failure. A few scientists associated with ARPANET later refuted this notion. That may be so, however survivability was always a key consideration because of the unreliable nature of network nodes and links in those days. The basis for the concept of packet switching—that is, forwarding of independent "message blocks"—ensures delivery of data despite network unreliability.

Additionally, subscribers make their own arrangements for Internet connectivity to the LinkedIn service. All data entered and saved by users is recorded in the LinkedIn database, and LinkedIn need not care about the state or operation of the intermediate network that connects its database to its subscribers. (Though I'm sure it does, for practical business reasons.)

However in the case of OSPF routers; there is no central routing database to which they can report route updates and that will perform route calculations for them. If a routing architect were to toy with the idea of creating such a central routing application, one that would single-handedly perform the task of building and maintaining updated routing tables for all the routers in a domain, then that architect also would have to figure out how those routers after initialization would know the right paths along which they can forward the network topology data to the central routing application. The situation is similar in the case of data originating from the central routing application but with a (naturally) unknown destination address further downstream. This path selection would have to be done despite the routers no longer ascertaining the network routes and despite the design trade-offs needed to make such a solution useful to customers.

Separate Yet Identical Databases

It should be obvious now why routers need to collect and maintain network topology information by themselves, and also to perform their own, independent determination of appropriate network paths to destinations. And, as mentioned above, the smart way for routers to know about destinations that are beyond their immediate circle of neighboring routers is to get that information from those neighboring routers. Because having a single, common topological database is not desirable, it is preferable that each router maintain its own database, which is nonetheless identical with the database of the others.

■ ■ ■

CHAPTER 14

The Enterprise Network— Recognizing the Neighbors

Men and Women walked casually about as they did on the main floor, every now and then stopping one another, exchanging pleasantries or scraps of relevantly irrelevant information. Gossip

—Robert Ludlam, *The Bourne Identity*

After two neighboring routers exchange "Hello" messages and agree on certain crucial parameters, they start exchanging network topology information. This chapter provides an overview of the kind of topology information exchanged between neighboring routers.

Link State Advertisements and Databases

When two neighboring routers discover each other and confirm bidirectional communications, as well as reach agreement on crucial parameters, the two routers then move on to the next stage in their neighborly relationship. This phase consists of building "full adjacency," and it involves exchanging network topology information consisting of records, each of which has been created or originated by a router in the domain.

That is, every router in a particular domain originates one record, listing its neighboring routers. The record acts as sort of an advertisement, announcing the directly connected destinations or routers[1st degree] of the originating router. This is called a *Link State Advertisement* (LSA).

Every router maintains a database that stores a current copy of its self-originated LSA, as well as the self-originated LSAs of other routers in the network, which it receives via its neighboring routers. This topological database is called the *Link State Database,* or LSA database. Similarly, when a router self-originates its LSA database, copies of that LSA database are released to its "adjacent" neighbors—that is, to its bidirectionally reachable neighboring routers. This is done as part of database synchronization.

The LSA Calling Card

A router's LSA describes the originating router's active links to its neighbors. The first four elements of information carried within that LSA are in the header:

- **The IP address of the originating router**. See Chapter 12's discussion of IP addresses.

It's an acknowledged reality that network links and other parts of networks are prone to failure, so incorporating temporal features in the information elements related to network states has always been considered crucial. For example:

- **Age field**: Any LSA has a so-called age field. When the originating router creates (self-originates) an LSA, its age is set to zero. Thereafter, the field is regularly incremented, regardless of whether it remains stored in the Link State Database of the same router or is copied, transmitted, and stored in the LSA database of some other router in that same domain.

Imagine the age field as a clock embedded in the LSA record that keeps ticking away relentlessly. The clock gets duplicated even when copies of the record are made, without losing a second; it never misses a beat, even when the record is getting transmitted.

The default maximum age for an LSA is a global parameter of 60 minutes. So, if any router finds that its LSA database has an LSA record that has reached 60 minutes, it is immediately purged from its database.

- **Sequence Number**: Every LSA has a field for holding an identifier called the *sequence number*. When a router's self-originating LSA reaches its maximum age naturally, or if it needs to be prematurely replaced because of changes in the router's neighborhood topology, the router creates a fresh LSA (with the latest topology details). The sequence number of the fresh LSA is set a unit higher than that of the earlier LSA. This sequence number remains constant during the itinerant lifetime of the LSA.

As always, the age of the fresh LSA starts off as zero, with increments thereafter. When a neighboring router receives this LSA, it looks at the sequence number and then at the age field, and it makes a comparison with any existing LSA it may have in its database that came from the same router.

- **Checksum**.

Another field in the LSA is:

- **Number of active router interfaces or links**.

Then, the following three elements of information might be repeated, depending on the number of active links (number of routers[1st degree]):

- **The IP address of the directly connected physical interface of the originating router**. This information gives identity information about the specific interface linked to a neighboring router.

- **The IP address of the directly connected neighboring router**. That is, the router[1st degree] and/or the network number of the directly connected stub network (st.network[1st degree]).

- **The Metric**. This is the cost associated with use of the router interface or link.

The header of an LSA may be considered as the visiting card of the LSA; a detachable identifier. On occasions when routers just need to inform or confirm to each other that they have shared LSAs, they exchange only the LSA headers (identifiers) instead of the entire LSAs. That's more efficient overall and is the method used during LSA database synchronization.

Database Synchronization

As mentioned, an LSA is considered the authoritative announcement by the originating router about the state of its links or interconnections with its neighboring routers. Only an originating router can withdraw its LSA prematurely from the domain. It does so by *reflooding* the LSA, albeit with its age prematurely set at maximum. On receiving that LSA, the other routers *flush* (remove) the LSA from their LSA databases. (More on this topic in later chapters; suffice it to say that this action is similar to what the term suggests.)

A recipient router typically removes from its own LSA database an LSA that originated from another router if:

- The LSA has reached maximum age. The router does a reflooding exercise on behalf of the seemingly "preoccupied" originating router so that the other routers in the network also flush out that LSA from their LSA databases.

- The LSA is found to be damaged; it discovers this through verification of its checksum.

- The LSA needs to be replaced by a more contemporary LSA that has been received from the same originating router.

LSA Exchanges vs. "Hello" Messages

The list of neighboring routers maintained by an LSA database might sound suspiciously similar to the list of neighboring routers that is part of those "Hello" messages regularly generated by any active router and that are received by its neighbors. Why the seeming duplication? Well, the purpose of a "Hello" message, along with its contents, is different from that of LSA communications.

The "Hello" message from a router contains a list of that router's detected neighbors. But the receiving router's immediate task, upon receiving the "Hello" message, is to determine whether that list mentions its own identifier or not. It is verifying its bidirectional communication with that originating router. Mention of other routers in the domain does not confirm bidirectional communication between them as well. That is, the receiving router cannot make that determination on behalf of the originating router. So, any mention of other routers in that "Hello" message is ignored. In contrast, the originating router's LSA lists its neighboring routers after bidirectional communications have been confirmed.

■ **Note**   "State" in network parlance refers to a defined stage in a controlled chain of events. In the case of LSA database communications, this means full adjacency with a neighboring router. In practical terms, "full adjacency" carries more significance than the words "connection up"; hence, there are a few additional elements of information in the LSA describing the state of the links of the originating router other than simply "up" and "down."

Bidirectional Communications

To illustrate how this bidirectional communication is established, let's construct the LSA for toothfix.genially.bhopal.router/24, the Bhopal router introduced in Chapter 12. In this example, we will assume that each of the links shown in the toothfix.genially.0.0/16 network has a unit cost associated with it in each direction. Traversing any single link in either direction gets counted as one hop—that is, one step. (This is similar to the "one hop/degree" concept we discussed in connection with LinkedIn.)

Overlooking the sequence, age, and checksum fields (updating the age field regularly is beyond us, in any case), we see that the Bhopal router has three active links with active routers at Chennai, Mumbai, and Delhi (recall Figure 12-1). We will assume that bidirectional adjacency has been established with each of them. Apart from these three connections, though, the router at Bhopal also has a direct link to a stub network—the LAN at Bhopal. That, too, is part of its neighborhood or topology, and needs to be advertised.

Because we know that this organizational network and its (sub)networks start with the network prefix toothfix.genially.0.0/16, I will skip using that in this example. So, the Bhopal router's LSA (neighbors[1st degree])will be as follows:

Originating router	no. of	Neighbor	Neighbor	Neighbor	Stub Network
bhopal.router	4	chennai.router	mumbai.router	delhi.router	bhopal.lan

Any change in the status of one of the links that appears in the above-announced LSA will result in the originating router's withdrawing that LSA and issuing a fresh, amended LSA with the new neighborhood topology details.

Failure and Recovery

A router is not interested in diagnosing failures. Any inability to communicate over a link is reason enough simply to red-flag it. That inability to communicate may be because of the link or a failure of the neighboring router port or administrator. Recovery is crucial in routing, but it is attained by routing around any points of failure and not by recovering points of failure. This seeming indifference to failure is reflected in the limited semantics of the routing protocol and the language used to explain it. Those who developed the OSPF protocol truly looked at things from the router's perspective!

There is one scenario in which the OSPF routing protocol falls a bit short of its hoary TCP/IP design principles: when a backbone area splits or gets partitioned. That's when the administrator needs to intervene to configure virtual links that act as a bridge for traffic to flow between those separated backbone partitions. However, even when parts of the autonomous system become isolated, nothing disturbs the active routers' rhythmic responses—whatever can be connected is connected, and that's that!

■ **Note**   Router devices close to the site of a failure are typically tasked to collect log data and send it across to a system that is used by the network/security administrator for correlation, analysis, and diagnosis. But none of these activities, including the collection of logs, is related to the routing protocol.

CHAPTER 15

■ ■ ■

Splitting the Autonomous System into Areas

The only real voyage of discovery consists not in seeking new landscapes, but in having new EYES.

—Marcel Proust

This chapter defines the reach of operations, or domain, of the routing protocol of a network and discusses how the domain is kept under control by network segmentation to ensure efficient use and management of resources.

The Autonomous System Split into Areas

The term *routing domain* has been liberally used until now without expressly defining it. Somewhere earlier, it was implied that a routing domain is the purview of the routing protocol. A more specific definition is in order now.

The domain of a routing protocol consists of all the routers that are running the same instance of the protocol and that are sharing the same routing information. Note that I do not use the word *exclusively* here because there could be a few edge routers that are part of more than one domain, so as to provide inter-domain connectivity.

All the routers in the domain of the routing protocol develop identical Link State databases. Distribution of Link State Advertisements for a domain's Link State database (topology information) occurs only within the domain and no further.

OSPF allows contiguous networks to be grouped together (or split). Each such group, together with the routers having interfaces to any one of the included networks, is called an *area*.

An autonomous system (AS) may be likened to a single administrative domain consisting of routers that run the same interior gateway routing protocol. For purposes of management and efficiency, as the AS grows in size, it makes sense to partition the domain into areas. This is how multiple instances of the protocol are run within the same AS: one instance per area, with each instance having its own, separate Link State database.

All the routers within one area are peers of a sort, because they share the same Link State information and they maintain identical Link State databases. If a router has interfaces to more than one area, then it maintains a separate Link State database for each of those areas it is connected to. Such a router is called an *Area Border Router* (ABR).

■ **Note** A router, by definition, routes between networks. It is likely to have interfaces in different networks. One or more of the networks may belong to the newly created areas. That explains the fussiness of references to router interfaces as "members of areas."

So, the segmentation of an AS into areas is not just physical; it's also logical in nature, with the peer routers in each area developing a detailed topology overview of just their own areas, which is not shared with the peer routers of other areas.

This setup is a lot like when a mapmaker splits a large, detailed, unwieldy map into smaller maps for the benefit of users (see Figure 15-1). But how does the viewer of one portion know how to assemble the various smaller maps to recreate the larger picture? Obviously, each small map needs to have some references to the connecting points on the other small maps. These references, or guidelines, make the task easier to join the pieces, or to find the right path that leads to the next leg of any cross-border journey. The path or road on one small map links up with its continuation on the next small map.

Figure 15-1. One of the ways of dividing a map into regions

In the same way, any traffic between a router source and a destination device located in a different area of an AS flows along a path that consists of, at minimum, the following components:

- an intra-area path within the source area

- an inter-area path traversing the source and the destination areas

- an intra-area path within the destination area

Thus, the peer routers in each area not only need to maintain detailed topology information about their own areas, but they also need to have some kind of condensed topology information about the areas with which they are expected to exchange inter-area traffic. This condensed information could be a route to an identified ABR for each contiguous group of visible, distant destination networks.

Therefore, there needs to be injection into one area of the condensed topology some information about those other areas. The points of *physical* intersection are the ABRs, which simultaneously maintain separate Link State databases for those different areas. Each ABR can summarize the information of one Link State database for injection into another.

Arrangement of the Areas

It is instinctive to split the AS into areas along boundaries created by edge routers that do not experience much cross-border traffic. Even so, any such segmentation has to follow certain topology guidelines to ensure that the areas are not *logically* isolated from each other and are not completely unaware of how to handle inter-area traffic. The designers of OSPF decided to choose a mandatory hub-and-spoke design, or backbone topology, for splitting and/or attaching the areas so as to maintain inter-area connectivity.

The Backbone, or Hub

There is a central area to which all the other areas get attached, which is referred to as the OSPF backbone. It is Area 0, often written as Area 0.0.0.0 (because OSPF area IDs are typically formatted as IP addresses). All the ABRs also belong to the backbone. In other words, the ABRs are located on the edge of the backbone.

Any traffic between two non-backbone areas has to necessarily flow through the intermediate backbone. It follows that the backbone must be physically contiguous. However, to account for contingencies, any physical separation can be overcome by configuring virtual links across non-backbone areas.

The Paths and Area Routers

The path between a source and a destination device located in a different area of an AS consists of the following components:

- an intra-area path within the source area, between the source device and an ABR

- a backbone path traversing the backbone, between the source ABR and the destination ABR

- an intra-area path within the destination area, between an ABR and the destination device

As mentioned, the backbone area is the central region, Area 0; all the other regions attach themselves to the backbone area and can reach each other only by going through the backbone.

When an AS is split into areas, the routers are functionally divided into the following categories, some of which overlap:

- **Internal Router**: The interfaces connect to networks belonging to the same area. This router maintains a single Link State database.

- **Area Border Router**: These routers belong to multiple areas, including the backbone area. An ABR runs multiple instances of the routing protocol, one for each attached area. Thus, it maintains multiple Link State databases. The ABR summarizes the information in the Link State databases of non-backbone areas for injection into the backbone. The backbone, in turn, distributes the information to the other areas.

- **Backbone Router**: This router has an interface to the backbone. It includes all ABRs, but there could also be routers inside the backbone that do not connect to other areas (i.e., they are not ABRs). Nevertheless, they belong to this category. (Such routers are both internal routers and backbone routers.)

- **AS Boundary Router**: This router exchanges routing information with routers outside the AS. It advertises AS external information throughout its system. AS boundary routers may be internal routers or ABRs.

Inter-Area Routing

Routes to destinations outside a source area are injected into that area by ABRs, which also belong to the backbone. The *route* essentially is the path from an ABR for a particular range of external destination IP addresses, which is expressed as a [address, mask] pair.

The cost of such a route is the maximum cost to any of the networks falling within the specified range. The appropriate ABR to use for a particular target area (if more than one is available) is selected in exactly the same way as is a route to an internal destination. The external routes to all destinations outside the area, advertised by the attached ABRs, are calculated.

Repair of Partitioned Areas

OSPF doesn't attempt to repair area partitions. When an area is partitioned, each component becomes a separate area, and the backbone performs routing between the new areas. Some destinations that are reachable via intra-area routing before the partition will then require inter-area routing.

However, to maintain routing after the partition, an address range must not be spread across multiple partitions. (This effectively results in multiple areas having the same address range. Imagine the confusion from a routing perspective!) Instead, smaller, contiguous, subnets are created for the newly created areas. Also, the backbone itself must not partition. If it does, parts of the AS become unreachable. Backbone partitions are repaired by configuring virtual links.

Domain Overview and Trust

A long look at Figure 15-2 reveals the AS's close hierarchy of trust. The backbone area is the most trusted, expected to be monitored by the most trusted administration. The ABRs belonging to the other areas are also part of the trusted backbone, and they are under the same administration. It is expected that the summary information those routers inject into the backbone, and that eventually reaches non-backbone areas, will be validated and able to be trusted.

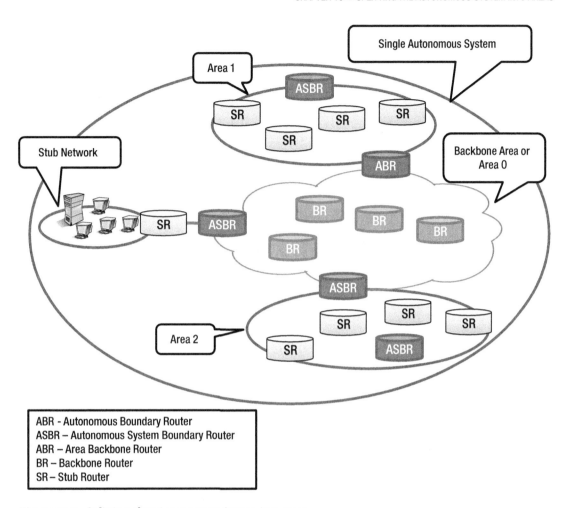

Figure 15-2. *Splitting of an Autonomous System into areas*

This figure shows the appropriate configuration that permits the routing protocol to be split into smaller areas, ensuring flexibility while maintaining the proper level of trust to propagate reasonably validated routing information.

CHAPTER 16

Link State Advertisements

Don't shrink your standards; link yourself with those who think and ink like you.

—Michael Bassey Johnson, poet and novelist

Every so often it helps to go back to the beginning and remind ourselves of the purpose of our efforts.

Our primary or eventual purpose is to devise a scheme that calculates the shortest or most efficient path between two distant routers in a network.

We determined in Chapter 13 why it is better suited for routers to perform their routing functions mostly independent of each other. We ascertained that every router needs to collate an independent but identical topological database. That in turn is later used to construct each router's own personalized view of the network, called the *routing table*.

In Chapter 14, we discussed the exchange of Link State Advertisements as part of the database exchange process. In Chapter 15 we learned how the administrative map of the AS is split into smaller areas to keep routing domains manageable and routing decisions efficient.

In this chapter, we describe the different kinds of Link State Advertisements—their formats and functions. This will give advanced readers insight into some of the details that the protocol has incorporated in its design apart from those of the simple case study considered in Chapter 14. The chapter concludes with an overview of LSAs.

The Role of Link State Advertisements

Network topology information is exchanged between two fully adjacent routers in the form of Link State Advertisements (LSA). In this chapter, the various types of LSAs are reviewed and the packet structure of each type is studied.

For a router to collate an objective topological map of the network that is identical to the ones assembled by others, it is obvious that every router needs to have the same pieces of the map. They need to gather the same pieces of the puzzle, if you will. Each piece has to be centered on a corresponding portion of the network and authoritatively described by the directly connected router.

An LSA is that piece. It is considered as the authoritative announcement by the originating router about the description of its connections with its neighborhood. All the LSAs, when collected together, form the Link State (LS) database. **The** *flooding process* ensures that every router in the same routing domain has the same collection of LSAs and, hence, an identical LS database. That is, every router has the same collective overview of the topology of the network.

■ **Note**   Flooding is the distribution of information throughout/within the network by means of selective multicasting. That is, a router releases an LSA (in an update packet) on all its interfaces except the one from which it was received. However, the LSA multicasting is limited to a hop of one. This is to force the neighboring routers to inspect the LSA and determine its status in their databases before choosing to either forward the LSA in a similar fashion or to disregard it.

An LSA needs to carry two kinds of information:

- Some sort of database recordkeeping information to uniquely identify it. This information is carried in the LSA header, whose format is common to all types of LSAs.

- Local network topology information that's being described by the originating router. This is the data payload carried in the body of the LSA. The body format is determined by the type of LSA.

The LSA Header

An LSA has a 20-byte header. Its format is common to all types of LSAs. This header contains enough information to uniquely identify the LSA. A router may come across multiple instances (versions) of an LSA at the same time. In any case, it can store only one instance, so it becomes necessary to determine which instance is more recent. This is accomplished by examining the LSA header. Figure 16-1 shows an LSA header. Now, let's review the fields in this header.

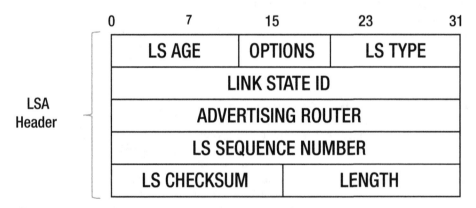

Figure 16-1. *LSA header*

LS Age

This is the time measured in seconds since the LSA was generated. The field is regularly incremented, as it remains stored in the Link State database of a router or even while it is copied and transmitted across the network.

Under normal circumstances, the LS age field does not exceed 30 minutes. If the age of an LSA reaches 30 minutes, the originating router refreshes the LSA by flooding a new instance of the LSA, with its LS sequence number incremented and its LS age set to zero again.

The age of an LSA is never incremented past its maximum limit (MaxAge) of 60 minutes. LSAs reaching MaxAge are not retained in the router's database. To ensure that an LSA at MaxAge is removed from the databases of all the domain routers at more or less the same time, without depending upon synchronized clocks, the MaxAge LSA is reflooded and all the routers remove their database copies.

The OSPF also allows premature aging of LSAs, thereby deleting an LSA from the routing domain without waiting for its LSA age to reach MaxAge. There might be occasions when a router wishes to delete a self-originated LSA instead of updating its contents. By setting the LS age field to MaxAge prematurely and reflooding the LSA, the router ensures that the self-originated LSA is deleted from the domain's distributed database.

A router may only prematurely age its own LSAs; it may not prematurely age LSAs originated by other routers.

A router may commence the flooding of its own self-originated LSA (newly issued, prematurely aged or Max Aged) or that of another router's LSA which has reached MaxAge. A router will, of course, commence flooding any LSA in its database which is requested by an adjacent neighbor during the database synchronization process.

Options

The options field of the header reveals the optional capabilities associated with the router originating the LSA. This field is present in a router's "Hello" packets, database description packets, and LSAs.

The same capabilities must be shared by all the routers attached to a specific area. A router will not accept a neighbor's "Hello" packet unless it has matching capabilities. An example of this is the ExternalRoutingCapability (the E-bit).

Certain OSPF areas are configured as "stubs." Information about AS external routes is not flooded into stub areas. This capability of the intervening area border routers to restrict such information is represented by the E-bit in the OSPF options field. To ensure consistent configuration of stub areas, every router interfacing to such an area must have the E-bit clear in its "Hello" packet.

■ **Note** The options field is present in "Hello" packets, data description packets, and LSA headers. The presence or use of the same bits of information at multiple stages indicates the possibility of assigning local significance to some bits for determining neighborhood relationships and global (domain) significance to the others for calculating routes.

LS Type

Let us consider some of the different kinds of LSAs that are originated. This book discusses only five types of LSAs. The first four are LSAs flooded within a single area only:

- *Type 1 Router LSAs*: Every router connects to network media or neighbors using active links. So every router needs to originate a topological description of its immediate neighborhood covered by its active links called a router LSA. Each describes the states of all the router's interfaces to an area. Certain routers are given additional responsibilities that further enhance their direct view of the network. They originate additional LSAs.

- *Type 2 Network LSAs*: A designated router connects to a network medium (e.g., Ethernet) along with other routers and holds special status among the multicast group. It is the record keeper of the group and hence is best qualified to know the list of all the fully adjacent routers directly connected to the network. So the DR of a broadcast network additionally originates a network LSA that contains the list of routers connected to the network.

- *Type 3 Summary LSAs*: Area Border Routers (ABRs) demarcate the boundary of the broadcast domain for the routing protocol. They assume the additional responsibility of advertising routes of distant networks that are not part of the area. Any ABR will originate LSAs describing one area's summary address information for injection into the backbone area, which lies within the same Autonomous System (AS). These are type 3 summary LSAs that describe routes to networks outside an associated area but within the same AS.

- *Type 4 Summary LSAs*: Area Border Routers also originate Type 4 summary LSAs describing routes to ASBRs. Summary LSAs are injected into the backbone by the ABR of an area that contains an ASBR. This ensures all other routers in the OSPF domain can reach the ASBR.

- *Type 5 AS-External LSAs*: These are originated by AS boundary routers and flooded unmodified throughout the AS, across all areas, except in stub areas. Each AS-external LSA describes a route to a destination network in another autonomous system and is otherwise also called a *default route*.

Every ABR maintains one separate, distinct Link State database for each area it connects to.

Link State ID

Based on the Link State Type, the Link State ID identifies the part of the routing domain that is being described by the LSA (see Figure 16-2). Depending on the LS type, the LS ID takes on the values listed in Table 16-1.

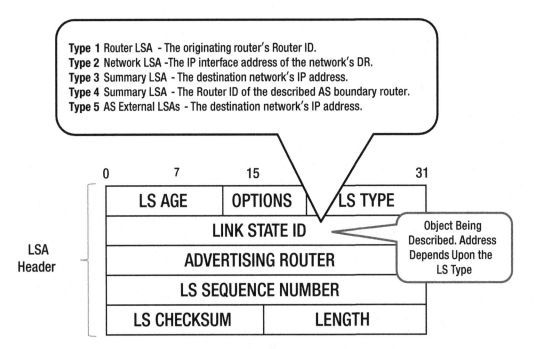

Figure 16-2. *LSA header*

Table 16-1. *LSA Types*

LS Type	LS Type	Distribution	Originating Router	Link State ID
1	Router LSA	Single area	Every router	Originating router's ID
2	Network LSA	Single area	DR of a network segment	The IP interface address of the network's designated router
3	Summary LSA (summarizing route to a destination outside the area but inside the AS)	Single area	ABR	The destination network's IP address
4	Summary LSAs (describing the route to an ASBR)	Single area	ABR	The Router ID of the described AS boundary router
5	AS external LSAs (describing the route to a destination in another AS)	AS, except stub areas	ASBR	The destination network's IP address

Since OSPF supports variable-length subnet masking (VLSM), a few bits of the host address may be "stolen" to create additional subnets.

■ **Note** For a router, the internal subnet details of a distant target network will be uninteresting. So this allows for supernetting! The router's primary objective will be to route packets to the destination network. Subsequent routing within the network will not be its concern.

When the LSA type is related to that of a network (LSA type = 2, 3, or 5), the network's IP address is easily derived by masking the LS ID with the network/subnet mask contained in the body of the LSA.

When the LSA type is related to that of a router (LSA type = 1 or 4), the LS ID is always the described router's OSPF router ID.

When an AS-external LSA (LSA type = 5) is describing a default route to any destination outside the AS, its LS ID is set to 0.0.0.0.

Advertising Router

This field identifies the OSPF router ID of the LSA's originator.

In the case of router LSAs, this field is identical to the LS ID field.

- Network LSAs are generated by the network's designated router.

- Summary LSAs are originated by area border routers.

- AS-external LSAs are originated by AS boundary routers.

LS Sequence Number

The sequence number field is a signed 32-bit integer. A router sets the initial sequence number at the smallest negative value the first time it originates any LSA. Afterwards, the router increments the LSA's sequence number each time it originates a new instance of the LSA. When an attempt is made to increment the sequence number past the maximum, that instance of the LSA must first be flushed from the routing domain. This is done by prematurely aging the LSA and reflooding it. Then a new instance can be originated with the sequence number reset at the initial sequence number of the smallest possible negative value.

■ **Note**   Routers are allowed to update only self-originated LSAs. It must be added that routers are not allowed to update their self-originated LSAs more than once every 5 seconds.

LS Checksum

This field is the checksum of the complete contents of the LSA, excepting the LS age field. The LS age field (2 bytes in length) is exempted so that an LSA's age can be incremented without updating the checksum.

The checksum is used to detect data corruption of an LSA. This corruption can occur while an LSA is being flooded in a Link State Advertisement or while it is being held in a router's memory as part of the Link State database. A corrupted LSA will simply be discarded by a router.

Calculation of the checksum is not optional. So the checksum field cannot have a value of zero.

Whenever the LS sequence number field notes that two instances of an LSA are identical, the LS checksum field is examined. If there is a difference, the instance with the larger LS checksum is considered to be most recent.

Length

The length field contains the length, in bytes, of the LSA, counting both LSA header (20 bytes long) and the data payload.

Comparing Two Instances of an LSA

When a router encounters two instances of an LSA, it must determine which is more recent. An LSA is identified by its LS type, ID, and LSA router. For two instances of the same LSA, the LS sequence number, LS checksum, and LS age fields are used to determine which instance is more recent (thereby accounting for all the header fields). As per the standard:

1.   The LSA having the newer LS sequence number is more recent.

2.   If the two instances have different LS checksums, then the instance having the larger LS checksum (when considered as a 16-bit unsigned integer) is considered more recent.

The Fletcher checksum (the algorithm used) has certain weaknesses. It cannot distinguish between blocks of all 0 bits and blocks of all 1 bits. This means a sequence of all 0 bytes has the same checksum as a sequence (of the same size) of all 1 bytes. One has to account for possibilities like these.

- If two instances have the same sequence numbers and checksum but if only one of the instances has its LS age field set to MaxAge (60 minutes), the instance of age MaxAge is considered to be more recent. Now both need to be gotten rid of! Remember that the LSA Age field has a limited length which results in a circular clock. The LSA instances deemed to be previous ones are discarded. The Max Age LSA is itself re-flooded. This forces the purging of the LSA from the databases of the routers in the domain.

- If the LS age fields of the two instances differ by more than 15 minutes, the instance having the younger LS age is considered to be more recent.

- Or else, the two instances are considered to be identical.

Router LSAs

A router LSA is a Type 1 LSA describing the state and cost of the entire router's links (interfaces). Every router originates a single router LSA, as shown in Figure 16-3. The LSA is flooded only within the area. The LSA describes the state and cost of the router's links (i.e., interfaces) to the area.

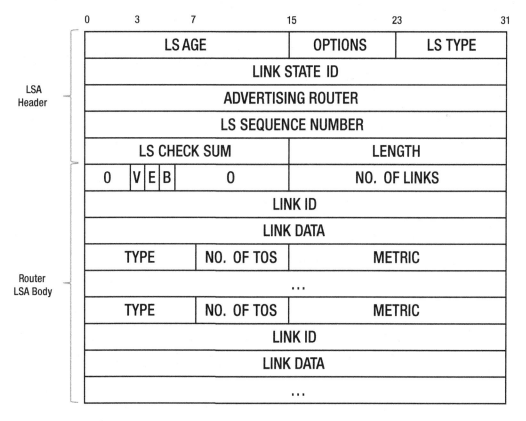

Figure 16-3. Router LSA

Link ID

The link ID is set to the originating router's OSPF router ID. (This will be similar to the Link State ID in the router LSA's header).

VEB

- *Bit-V*: This bit is set when the router is an endpoint of one or more fully adjacent virtual links (V, for *virtual*).

- *Bit-E*: This bit is set when the router is an AS boundary router (E, for *external*).

- *Bit-B*: This bit is set when the router is an area border router (B, for *border*).

Number of Links

This gives the count of router links (interfaces) in the area.

Link Description

The following fields are used to describe each router link (i.e., interface) and each router link is categorized by type. The type field indicates the kind of link being described.

Type Field

This describes the router link. Interestingly, host routes are classified as links to stub networks. See Table 16-2.

Table 16-2. *Possible Values of Type Field in the Router LSA Body*

Type	Description
1	Point-to-point connection to another router
2	Connection to a transit network
3	Connection to a stub network
4	Virtual link

■ **Note** *The values of all the other fields describing a router link depend on the link's type.*

Link ID Field

This identifies the entity to which the router link connects to. The value depends on the link's type. When connecting to an entity that also originates an LSA (i.e., another router or a transit network), the link ID is equal to the neighboring object's LSA State ID. This provides the index for looking up the neighboring LSA in the LS database.

Link Data Field

Each link has an associated 32-bit link data field. Its value depends on the link's type field. For connections to stub networks, the link data field specifies the network's IP address mask. For other link types, it specifies the router interface's IP address, which is needed when building the routing table, to calculate the IP address of the next hop.

Number of TOS Field

This is the number of TOS metrics for this link, not counting the required link metric. Therefore, if no additional TOS metrics are given, this field is set to zero.

Metric Field

This is the cost of using this router link.

TOS Options Field

Additional TOS-specific information can be included for backward compatibility with previous versions of the OSPF specification.

Router LSA Overview

Figure 16-4 provides an overall look at the router LSA body.

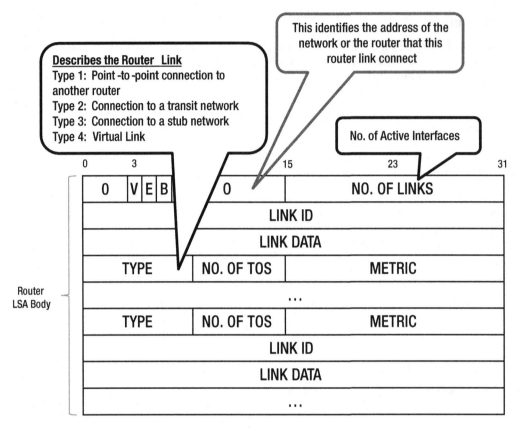

Figure 16-4. *Router LSA body*

The Router LSA highlights the different kinds of information that the designers of the protocol sought to pack into each type of LSA.

Despite having defined separate LSAs for those originated by ABRs and ASBRs, the Router LSA has bits to identify if the originating router is an ABR or ASBR.

Then the designers had to consider the different kinds of logical entities that a router could directly connect to. One would like to think that a router eventually connects to a router or does not, and that's that. But one needs to identify the type of link (broadcast network, point-to-point link, etc.) directly connected to a router's interface. It determines that nature of the network on that interface. Hence, the Type field in the Router LSA body and the corresponding Link ID fields.

Network LSAs

Network LSAs are type 2 LSAs (see Figure 16-5). The network's designated router originates a network LSA for each broadcast network in the area by. The network LSA lists all the routers attached to the network, including the designated router.

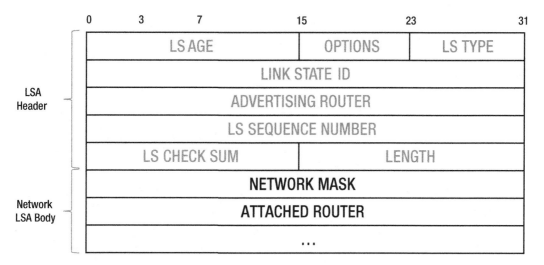

Figure 16-5. *Network LSA*

The LSA's Link State ID field lists the IP interface address of the designated router. There are no metrics fields present in the network LSA since the distance from the network to all attached routers is zero. Let's study the major elements of the network LSA.

Network Mask

This is the IP address mask for the network.

Attached Router

This lists the router IDs of those routers attached to the network that are fully adjacent to the designated router. The designated router itself is included in this list. The number of routers included can be calculated from the LSA header's length field. *Network LSAs are flooded throughout a single area only.*

Summary LSAs

Summary LSAs are the type 3 and type 4 LSAs that are *originated by area border routers* (see Figure 16-6). Summary LSAs summarize routes to destinations outside the area but within the AS. These LSAs are flooded throughout the associated areas.

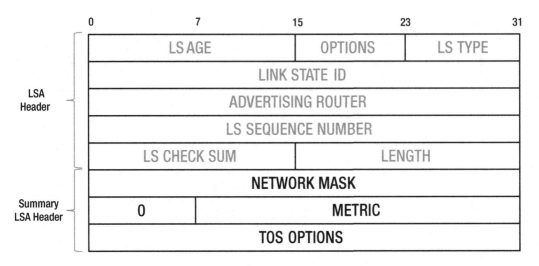

Figure 16-6. *Summary LSA*

Type 3 summary LSAs are used when the destination is an IP network: the LSA's ID field is an IP network number.

Type 3 summary LSAs can also be used to describe a default route for the benefit of stub areas. A default summary route is used in a stub area instead of flooding a complete set of external routes. When describing a default summary route, the summary LSA's LS ID is always set to DefaultDestination (0.0.0.0) and the network mask is set to 0.0.0.0.b.

A type 4 summary LSA is used when the destination is an AS boundary router. The LS ID field is the AS boundary router's OSPF router ID.

Other than the difference in the LS ID field, the format of type 3 and type 4 summary LSAs is identical.

Network Mask

For type 3 summary LSAs, this gives the destination network's IP address mask. The field is zero for type 4 summary LSAs.

Metric Field

This is the cost of this route, expressed in the same unit as the interface cost in the router LSA.

TOS Options Field

Additional TOS-specific information may be included, for backward compatibility with previous versions of the OSPF specification.

AS-External LSAs

AS-external LSAs are the type 5 LSAs (see Figure 16-7). AS boundary routers originate these LSAs and each describes a destination external to the AS. The LS ID field in such an LSA specifies an IP network number. AS-external LSAs are also used to describe default routes. The LS ID is always set to `DefaultDestination` (0.0.0.0) and the network mask is set to 0.0.0.0.

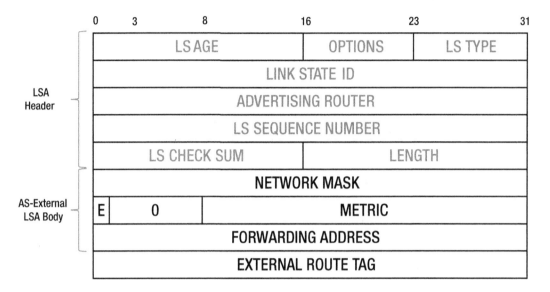

Figure 16-7. *AS-external LSA*

These LSAs are flooded throughout the AS (except for stub areas).

Network Mask

This is the IP address mask for the advertised destination.

Bit-E Field

This is the type of external metric. If bit-E is set, the metric specified is a type 2 external metric. If bit-E is zero, the specified metric is a type 1 external metric.

Metric Field

This is the cost of this route. Its interpretation depends on the setting of the E-bit above.

METRIC CLASSIFICATION

There are four classifications for metrics in terms of preference. In terms of decreasing preference, these are:

- Intra-area

- Inter-area

- External type 1: a summation of the internal path costs to the ASBR that advertises the route followed by the external path cost to the final destination. The external path costs are measured using the same metrics as the internal path costs.

- External type 2: its value is solely that of the external path cost. External type 2 metrics assumes that routing between ASs is the major cost of routing a packet. This means there is no need to consider internal link state metrics.

Forwarding Address Field

Data traffic for the destination external to the AS is directed to this address (presumably another ASBR). If the forwarding address is set to 0.0.0.0, data traffic will instead be led to the LSA's originator.

External Route Tag Field

This is a 32-bit field attached to each external route. It is not used by the OSPF protocol itself.

Supporting Stub Areas

AS-external LSAs are not flooded into stub areas. Routing to destinations outside the AS in these areas is based on default only. The stub area's area border router must advertise a default route for an AS external destination into the stub area via summary LSAs. These are flooded throughout the stub area, but no further. This ensures that the LS database size in the stub area remains within manageable limits and that routing decisions are efficient.

Virtual links cannot be configured through stub areas. This means that AS boundary routers cannot be placed internal to stub areas.

Chapter Summary

Table 16-3 summarizes the types of LSAs that have been presented in this chapter.

Table 16-3. *Different Types of LSAs Distributed by Different Kinds of Routers*

	Advertising Router (Originating Router)	Type of LSA	Distribution	Link State ID	Address of Network/Router in the Neighborhood
1	Any router	Router LSA	Single area	The originating router's ID	Neighboring router's ID (for a point-to-point connection to another router)
					IP address of designated router (for connection to a transit network)
					IP network/subnet number (for connection to a stub network)
					Neighboring router's ID (for connection to a virtual link)
2	Designated router (DR)	Network LSA	Single area	The IP interface address of the network's DR.	Router ID of the DR and all the other routers in the network fully adjacent to the DR
3	Area border router (ABR)	Type 3 summary LSA (summarizes the route to a destination outside the area and yet inside the AS, i.e., an inter-area route)	Single area	The destination network's IP address	Network mask included
4		Type 4 summary LSA (describes route to an ASBR)	Single area	The router ID of the described AS boundary router	[This field is meaningless]
5	Autonomous system boundary router (ASBR)	AS-External LSAs (describes route to destination in another AS)	AS, except stub areas	The destination network's IP address	Network mask included

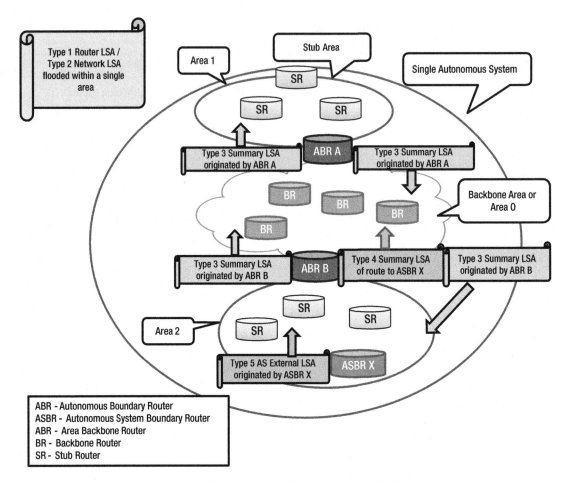

Figure 16-8. *Logical representation of the movement of LSAs across area border routers*

CHAPTER 17

The Enterprise Network–
Neighborhood Activity

"You are not playing the game" he said grimly. "English Gossip isn't supposed to get back to the person it's about."

—Elaine Dundy, *The Old Man and Me*

This chapter offers a quick overview of the processes implemented for the exchange of Link State Advertisements (LSA) for achieving synchronization of all LSA databases in the routers in the network domain.

The LSAs are exchanged between routers while encapsulated inside various kinds of OSPF messages (see later discussion of packets). Neighboring routers exchange the LSAs via two processes: *database synchronization* and *flooding*. The objective of these exercises is to quickly build and maintain identical LSA databases in the network routing domain that contain a copy of each router's latest LSA.

The routers are expected to achieve this synchronization and flooding before they start forwarding and receiving the end-user traffic (source–destination message movement). If they were to start forwarding this traffic before all the routers had identical maps of the network, all hell would break loose.

Imagine, for example, if router A forwarded a packet to router B, expecting B to forward it to router C. As per router A's calculations, router B lies next along the most appropriate path to destination router C. But router B has other calculations! Instead, it forwards the packet to router A, and you have the beginnings of a routing loop!

That's why there is obsessive focus on ensuring that all routers in a network domain have identical LSA databases.

Synchronization

Synchronization is undertaken right after there's confirmation of bidirectional communication between two neighboring routers. Presumably, that new neighbor was discovered when the router newly joined the network or when it rejoined the network after a failure. Especially in a case of a failure, you have to assume that the router could have missed a few LSA updates, so thorough verification is necessary.

At this point, the two neighboring routers synchronize their databases. However, instead of their exchanging entire databases, they engage in a more efficient exercise called *database exchange*. To be more precise, they are in a *database exchange state* (see Note on use of "state" in Chapter 14). Here's what happens:

1. Each router sends to the other router only the headers of the LSAs in its LSA database. The routers are said to be "describing their databases" using special database description packets, each of which carries multiple LSA headers.

2. The routers request from each other only those LSAs missing their own LSA databases or those LSAs superseded by more recent releases. This request is made using special LSA request packets, which also contain (multiple) LSA headers.

3. The requests are fulfilled by means of flooding, using LSA update packets that carry the requested LSAs.

The transmitted LSAs need to be individually acknowledged by the routers. As mentioned, the LSA headers are used for explicit acknowledgments; however, each acknowledgement need not be sent in a separate message. The packets are used for explicit acknowledgments; they are called LSA packets, each of which contains multiple LSA headers.

▪ **Note**   There are occasions when explicit acknowledgment is not worth the effort—that is, when the router does not have any other LSA packets to send to a neighboring router, and instead sends one or more LSA update packets. In this case, an implicit acknowledgment of the received LSA makes more sense. The router sends a copy of the same LSA as received (instead of just the header) along with the LSAs requested by the neighboring router in a scheduled LSA update packet.

Flooding

The network topology consists of the arrangement (graphical layout) of neighborhood routers—that is, the "local states" of all the routers, which includes their active interfaces and reachable neighbors (routers[1st degree]). Each of those neighboring routers in turn forwards the same LSA, without making any alterations, to all its neighboring routers except the one originating the LSA.

▪ **Note**   Another routing protocol, called Routing Internet Protocol (RIP), is often referred to as "routing by rumor" because of the subjective nature of the topology information that is shared. In RIP, any router passes "hearsay" topology information to the rest of its neighbors after interpreting the information it has received (a bit like the game of telephone). This is in contrast to OSPF, whereby unaltered topology (LSAs) is shared across a network without the intermediate routers introducing any changes.

Flooding, then, is the process by which these amended or newly released LSAs are distributed throughout the network domain. Every router in the network domain receives them, thereby ensuring that the LSA databases of all routers in the network domain are identical. The outcome of flooding, thus, is that all the routers are synchronized; this stage is popularly called *convergence*.

With convergence, the flooded LSA is thereafter refreshed (re-released) by the originating router every 30 minutes as part of its upkeep activity, ensuring that everything stays uniform and active. If there are any changes in the network, the originating router releases an amended LSA.

The Packets

Although the LSAs themselves flood the routers in the network domain, the update packets only get exchanged across adjacent routers. Thus, the LSA is unpacked from the update packet, examined, undergoes a series of operations, is copied, and then is repackaged in a fresh LSA update packet that is sent to all neighboring routers except the one that initiated it.

Now, let's consider all those different kinds of packets. OSPF has five different kinds:

1. "Hello" packets

2. Database description packets

3. LSA request packets

4. LSA update packets

5. LSA acknowledgement packets

Each of these packets carries specific fields, many of which are common fields, as should now be obvious. Four of the packet types carry headers of multiple LSAs.

All five packet types are themselves carried within a generic OSPF packet. The OSPF packet has a header (what's new?) with a few standard field sets. Three of these field sets are:

- The OSPF version, current version being version 2.0.

- Area ID, which is the ID of the routing domain to which the router belongs.

- Router ID, which is the ID of the router sending the OSPF packet. (This may not necessarily be the router originating the LSA—that is, there might be an LSA somewhere deep inside the packet.) The originating LSA router is identified in the LSA header.

The OSPF packet itself is carried in a standard IP packet/datagram. Russian dolls, anybody?

CHAPTER 18

OSPF Messages

Beginning of the teaching for life,

The instructions for well-being . . .

Knowing how to answer one who speaks,

To reply to one who sends a message.

—Amenemope, Egyptian pharaoh, c.1100 B.C.E

Various kinds of OSPF messages are exchanged between routers in the process of synchronizing their Link State databases. This Database Exchange Process is reviewed in this chapter, including a description of the types of messages sent in a simple network and the modifications that are made for application to a larger Ethernet system, especially for multicasting/broadcasting.

The Types of Messages Sent

Once two neighboring routers have established bi-directional communication, they commence initializing the next stage of message processing, leading to what is called *full adjacency*. Before full adjacency is achieved, the routers are simply termed *adjacent*.

It is during this phase that they start synchronizing their current Link State databases. Once that synchronization is completed, the two routers are ready to exchange Link State Advertisements (LSAs) that are flooded, as subsequent changes occur in the area network's topology.

In addition to the "Hello" packets discussed in an earlier chapter, OSPF has four other kinds of messages, each with its own packet. These packets are:

- **Database Description**: When initializing an adjacency between two neighboring routers, OSPF exchanges database description packets, which list the contents of the topological database.

- **Link-State Request**: While parsing the received description packets, if a router detects that portions of its topological database need to be updated, it sends a Link-State request packet to its neighbor, asking for the specific LSAs that are missing or that need replacement.

- **Link-State Update:** These packets carry one or more LSAs going one hop from their originating router to a neighboring router. The originating router multicasts (floods) these packets if the network supports such a multicast or broadcast mode.

- **Link-State Acknowledgment:** The receiving router sends an LSA acknowledgment packet in reply to any LS update packets it has received, so as to confirm that the update packets have been received successfully.

Now, let's take a closer look at these packets.

The Database Description Packet

Database description packets are OSPF packet type 2, as shown in Figure 18-1.

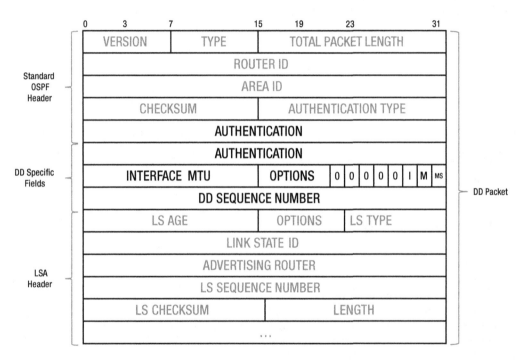

Figure 18-1. *The data description packet*

Each router uses these packets to list all the LSAs present in its Link State database. Multiple packets may be used to catalog the database. The objective of this exchange of packets by two neighboring routers at this stage is to inform each other of the contents of their respective databases, and not to swap the databases per se. So these packets carry just the headers of the LSAs the sending router has in its database. This saves space.

As shown in Figure 18-1, each description packet consists of the OSPF header, the packet sequence number, and multiple LSA headers. When the neighboring router notices an LSA that is more recent than what it has in its own database, it requests this newer LSA. Talk about keeping up with the Joneses next door!

Fields in the Description Packet

The following fields appear in this packet:

- *Interface MTU*: This is the maximum size of IP datagram that can be sent to the associated interface, without fragmentation, in bytes. The interface MTU should be set to 0 in packets sent over virtual links.

- *Options*: This is the optional capabilities supported by the router.

- *I-bit*: This stands for "Init bit"; it is the first in the sequence of database description packets it is when set to 1.

- *M-bit*: This stands for "More bit." A value of 1 indicates that more database description packets are to follow.

- *MS-bit*: This stands for "Master/Slave bit." A value of 1 indicates that the router is the master during the database exchange process; otherwise, the router is the slave.

- *DD sequence number*: This is used to number the database description packets.

Roles of Slave and Master

To avoid the need for keeping track of two exchange (sequence) counters, the Database Exchange Process uses a master/slave relationship. This aspect comes into play via the database description packet (called DD in the figures that follow).

To begin, each router generates an empty data description packet (with no LSA headers) that has a unique sequence number and has the I, M, and MS bits set—essentially both are trying to insist on being the master. However, the router with the lower router ID concedes to the other, accepting its status as slave; the slave does this by sending an empty data description packet to the master router with the I and MS bits set at 0, but with the M bit set at 1. (See Figure 18-2.)

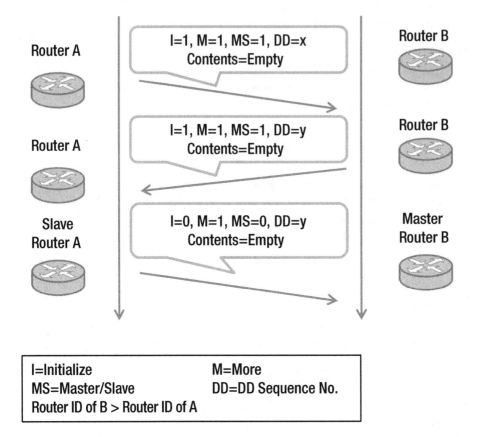

Figure 18-2. *Initial exchange of database description packets*

The master then generates the first "loaded" data description packet, summarizing part of its Link State database in the form of LSA headers. The database description packet's sequence number is incremented above its previous value by 1, as shown in Figure 18-3.

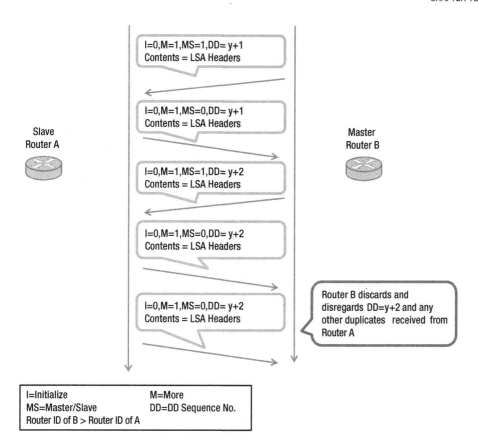

Figure 18-3. *Second exchange of database description packets*

The slave then sends its own database description packet listing its own Link State database while also acknowledging receipt of the master's database description packet; it does that by echoing the sequence number. (See Figure 18-4.) Only one data description packet is allowed to be pending at any one time.

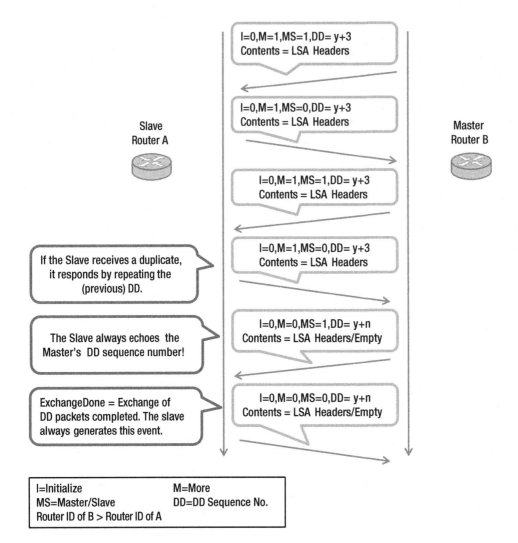

Figure 18-4. *Third exchange of data description packets*

Note that only the master router is allowed to retransmit database description packets. It does so at fixed intervals, the length of which is defined by using the per-interface constant RxmtInterval.

When the two neighboring routers have decided who is master and who is slave, and they have started exchanging database description packets, they are free to simultaneously exchange Link State request packets and Link State update packets. So to be honest, the Database Exchange Process can and does include not only the database description activity (exchange of LSA headers) but also the exchange of requested LSAs.

Link State Request Packet

The Link State request packets are OSPF packet type 3, as shown in Figure 18-5.

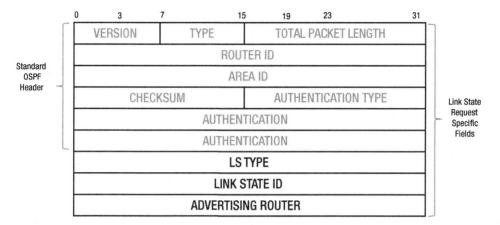

Figure 18-5. The Link State request packet

After (or while) the neighboring routers have been exchanging database description packets, one of them may find that parts of its LS database need updating. The Link State request packet, then, is used to request those pieces of a neighbor's database that are more up to date.

As shown in Figure 18-5, the request packet consists of the OSPF header plus portions of the LSA headers. Each LSA request is identified by its LS type, Link State ID, and LSA router. Note that while the LSA header in the database description packet has the age and checksum fields, the LS request packet is bereft of them.

It is assumed that the LS request is for the most recent instance of the LSA, so that's not surprising. The database description packet has the needed details because the receiving router does the comparison. But when the need for a more recent instance of the LSA is determined, the source router has no option but to send the most recent instance of the LSA, since it does not store multiple instances of the same LSA. Hence, there's no need for redundant fields in the LSA request packet.

The Link State Update Packet

Link State update packets are OSPF packet type 4, as shown in Figure 18-6.

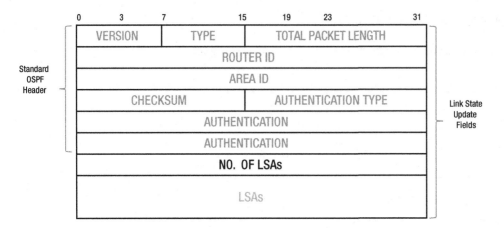

Figure 18-6. *The Link State update packet*

Link State update packets implement the flooding of LSAs, because several LSAs may be included in a single packet. The update packets travel one hop from their originating router.

The update packets are made up of the OSPF header plus the following fields:

- *Number of advertisements*: This is the number of LSAs included in the particular packet.

- *Link State Advertisements*: That is, the LSAs themselves.

The update packets are multicast on those physical networks that support multicasting or broadcasting. They get sent to all the routers in the multicast group, not just the one that made the LS request. In this way, the system periodically ensures that all the routers' databases are synchronized.

To make the flooding procedure reliable, flooded LSAs are acknowledged in the LS acknowledgment packets. If it is necessary to retransmit any LSAs, the retransmitted LSAs are always sent directly to the particular neighboring router.

The Link State Acknowledgment Packet

The Link State acknowledgment packets are OSPF packet type 5, as shown in Figure 18-7.

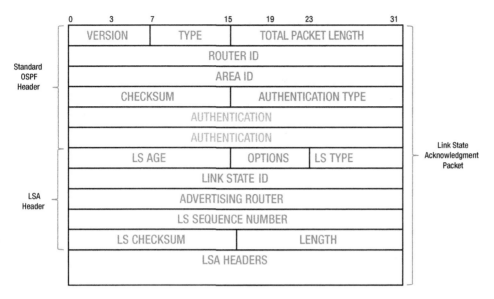

Figure 18-7. *The Link State acknowledgment packet*

For any flooding of LSAs to be reliable, each newly transmitted LSA must be acknowledged, and this is accomplished via the Link State acknowledgment packet. Multiple LSAs can be acknowledged in a single LS acknowledgment packet. The format of this packet is similar to that of the database description packet; the body of both packets is simply a list of LSA headers.

Explicit acknowledgments are typically time-delayed, thereby enabling multiple acknowledgments to be packaged in that single LS acknowledgement packet. This also permits a single LS acknowledgment packet to confirm acknowledgments to several other neighbors at the same time.

In this way, a sending router that receives an acknowledgment packet from a neighboring router will not be surprised to see acknowledgments for LSAs that it never sent! Nevertheless, that router is keeping track of the exchanges between neighboring routers (if it is part of a multicast group). In a sense, the acknowledgment process is a repeat of the Database Exchange Process, in that it has a similar packet format.

Networks that support multicasting, or broadcasting, have two router groups: `AllSPFRouters` and `AllDRouters`. Delayed acknowledgments are delivered based on the state of the transmitting interface. If the transmitting interface state is a designated router or its backup (more about designated routers in the next section), the destination `AllSPFRouters` is used; in all other states, the destination `AllDRouters` is used. On nonbroadcasting networks, though, the delayed acknowledgment packets must be unicast separately to each adjacent router.

Should a router receive duplicate LSAs, the explicit LS acknowledgments are sent directly to the concerned source router without further ado.

Acknowledgments can also be accomplished implicitly by adding the few pending acknowledgments as LSAs in otherwise pending LS update packets that are *directly addressed* to the same neighboring router. This is an alternative to sending them in separate acknowledgment packets.

Full adjacency is achieved upon completion of the Database Exchange Process and when all LS requests have been satisfied. The databases are then deemed synchronized, and the routers are marked as fully adjacent. The adjacency is fully functional, and the status is advertised in the two routers' router LSAs.

■ **Note**   At the beginning of the Database Exchange Process, two adjacent routers are said to be merely adjacent, versus fully adjacent.

The Designated Router and Its Backup

At this point, we know that two directly connected routers, on a point-to-point link, form full adjacency and can exchange LSAs so as to synchronize their databases. But on a shared Ethernet network of, say, six routers, a total of 15 adjacencies will need to be formed among those six routers (as shown in Figure 18-8). For 10 routers, there will be 45 adjacencies and corresponding database synchronizations required. Thus, there is the problem of creating a meshed network between n nodes; there needs to be nx(n-1)/2 distinct connections or links.

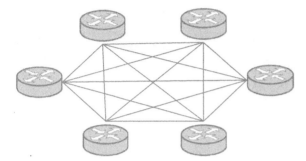

Figure 18-8. *Adjacencies required in a shared Ethernet network with six routers*

You can imagine the amount of traffic flowing in these complex networks, with the database description packets, request packets, and update and acknowledgment packets being sent back and forth, all of them flowing over a shared network—that would create a traffic pile-up.

However, here's where the designated and backup routers come to the rescue. Instead of each router's needing to form and maintain adjacencies with every other neighboring router on the network, one of the routers gets elected as designated router (DR). Its task is to keep track of the LSA updates and to assist the other routers in keeping their Link State databases synchronized. It does that via its own updated Link State database. The DR is also responsible for generating and flooding the LSAs for the neighborhood (the network).

Additionally, another router is elected as a backup, and it is called the backup designated router (BDR). See Figure 18-9 for a typical setup.

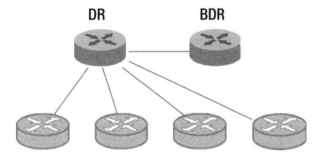

Figure 18-9. *Adjacencies required when there is a DR and a BDR*

The advantage of the DR/BDR system is that the routers need not form and maintain adjacencies with all the neighboring routers on a network. Instead, they do so only with the DR and the BDR. For example, for 10 routers, instead of 45 adjacencies in a meshed network, there are 17 adjacencies that are formed and maintained. As shown in Figure 18-10, for the six routers in a network, only nine adjacencies are required when a DR and BDR are utilized.

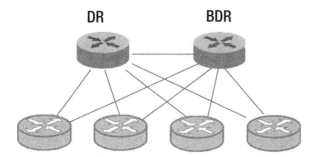

Figure 18-10. *Adjacencies when there's a DR and a BDR in a shared network with broadcasting capability*

The multicasting feature on a shared Ethernet thus permits the BDR to operate in silent mode. It listens to all the conversations addressed to the AllDRouters group (224.0.0.6) and AllSPFRouters group (224.0.0.5), thereby reducing the need for full adjacencies even further to (n-1).

■ **Note** Figure 18-10 is a logical representation of adjacencies in a group of routers connected to a shared network with multicasting/broadcasting support. It is not the logical representation of a network topology for the shared Ethernet network, which is typically shown to be a bit different. If it helps understanding, imagine Figure 18-10 as an overlay on the Layer2 representation of an Ethernet network.

CHAPTER 19

■ ■ ■

An Enterprise Network — Convergence of Data

In small towns, news travels at the speed of boredom.

—Carlos Ruiz Zafón

Using the example of the organization-wide network detailed in Chapter 12, we can observe how changes in the topology of one part of a network results in a cascade of information to all other parts of the network, which then culminates in a resynchronization of the Link State databases of all the routers in the network. But let's take a closer look at how that synchronization is achieved.

The Synchronization of Routers

Using the Chapter 12 organizational network as our basis, let's see how long it takes for the router in Bhopal to learn about the "network routes" to the router in Seattle (see Figure 19-1). For that to happen, the Bhopal router will need to acquire the LSA of any other router with links to the Seattle router—that is, the Chicago router or the Boston router.

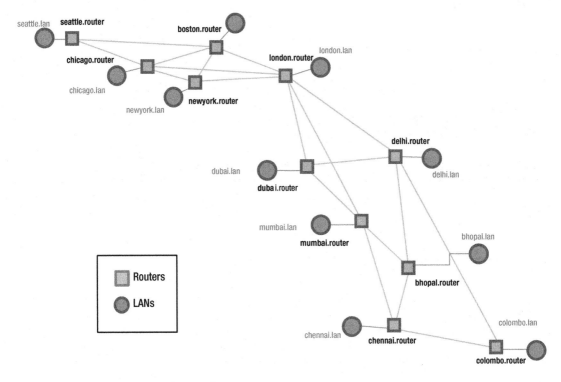

Figure 19-1. *An organizational network*

Let's start from the beginning. We assume that all the routers are powered on at roughly at the same time (probably the ones in India a shade earlier). The Bhopal router goes through the regular routine of sending "Hello" greetings on its interfaces, and it thereby establishes bi-directional relationships with its three neighboring routers. By virtue of the manual configuration by the administrator, the router also knows that it has a stub network directly connected to it. So it then constructs its LSA from its newly populated neighbor database and loads it into its Link State database.

The Bhopal router's LSA (neighbors[1st degree]) is as follows:

Originating router	no. of links	Neighbor	Neighbor	Neighbor	Stub Network
bhopal.router	4	chennai.router	mumbai.router	delhi.router	bhopal.lan

The Mumbai router's LSA (neighbors[1st degree]) is:

Originating router	no. of links	Neighbor	Neighbor	Neighbor	Neighbor	Stub Network
mumbai.router	5	chennai. router	bhopal. router	dubai. router	london. router	mumbai. lan

The Chennai router's LSA (neighbors[1st degree]) is:

Originating router	no. of links	Neighbor	Neighbor	Neighbor	Stub Network
chennai.router	4	bhopal.router	mumbai.router	colombo.router	chennai.lan

The Delhi router's LSA (neighbors[1st degree]) is:

Originating router	no. of links	Neighbor	Neighbor	Neighbor	Neighbor	Stub Network
delhi.router	5	colombo. router	bhopal. router	dubai .router	london. router	delhi. lan

---

■ **Note**   Any stub network will initially look like the odd man out in an LSA and Link State database. The stub network is a passive entity in the landscape of routing (by virtue of its definition). But that does not render it unimportant, because it is nevertheless a part of the network. Its interconnecting router takes the responsibility of advertising its presence (route) in the domain and of acting as a bridge or proxy to the rest of the network domain. So, do not be puzzled if stub networks do not advertise their own LSAs, despite figuring in the LSAs of routers! You'll see their proxy routers doing that job for them.

Let's now look at what happens next.

- **1st Count** (after "Hello"): There is database exchange between Bhopal and (Mumbai, Delhi, Chennai).

That is, the Bhopal router synchronizes its Link State database with the databases of its three neighboring routers. When the synchronization is complete, the Bhopal router's Link State database is populated with four LSAs: three LSAs of its neighboring routers and one self-originated LSA. Bhopal's neighboring routers similarly receive the LSAs of their other neighbors.

- **1st Count (after "Hello"):** There is database exchange between (Dubai, Mumbai, Delhi) and London.

While synchronizing their Link State databases with the Bhopal router, the routers at Dubai, Mumbai, and Delhi are also synchronizing with the London router. When synchronization is complete, all three (Dubai, Mumbai, Delhi) have the London router's LSA in their LS databases.

- **1st Count (after "Hello"):** There is database exchange between Chicago and London.

In the meanwhile, at the other end, the Chicago router's LSA (neighbors[1st degree]) is:

Originating router	no. of links	Neighbor	Neighbor	Neighbor	Neighbor	Stub Network
chicago.router	5	seattle. router	newyork. router	boston. router	london. router	chicago. lan

The London router's LSA (neighbors[1st degree]) is:

Originating router	no. of links	Neighbor	Neighbor	Neighbor	Neighbor	Neighbor	Neighbor	Stub Network
london. router	7	chicago. router	newyork. router	boston. router	delhi. router	dubai. router	mumbai. router	london.lan

After database exchange with the Chicago router, the London router's Link State database comes into possession of the LSA of the Chicago router (as part of London's neighbors[2nd degree]).

- **2nd Count (after "Hello"):** There is database exchange between London and (Dubai, Mumbai, Delhi).

The London router floods the Chicago router's LSA. The Dubai, Delhi, and Mumbai routers receive copies. All three send back Link State acknowledgement packets to the London router, confirming their receipt of the Chicago router's LSA.

- **3rd Count (after "Hello"):** There is database exchange between London and (Dubai, Mumbai, Delhi).

After performing necessary operations on the received LSA, the routers at Dubai, Mumbai, and Delhi flood the Chicago router's LSA. The LSAs from Mumbai and Delhi are received by Bhopal and duly acknowledged. The Bhopal router in turn performs standard operations, and then it forwards the Chicago router's LSA only to Chennai (avoiding sending the LSA back to the routers from which it received the LSA).

So the Bhopal router receives the Chicago router's LSA, which contains a direct network route to Seattle, on the 3rd Count (after "Hello"). After another count, the Bhopal router receives the Seattle router's LSA.

That's the amount of time it is likely to take in this network, for the databases of the Bhopal router and the Chicago router to become identical—for news about a change in the Bhopal router's neighborhood to reach the Chicago Router, or vice versa.

Time of Convergence: *The amount of time required for the databases of all the routers in the domain to become identical.*

■ **Note** The above narrative did not account for the simultaneous (independent) flow of information taking place in all the other directions—that is, the exchanges of the other LSAs.

Table 19-1 shows the Link State database that would be present in every router when convergence is achieved. The database consists of the LSAs of all the routers—that is, it shows the neighbors[1st degree] of every router in the network.

Table 19-1. *Identical Link State Databases of All Routers in the Domain at Convergence: Neighbors[1st degree] of each router*

Originating router	no. of links	Neighbor	Neighbor	Neighbor	Neighbor	Neighbor	Neighbor	Stub Network
bhopal. router	4	chennai. router	mumbai. router	delhi. router				bhopal. lan
mumbai. router	5	chennai. router	bhopal. router	dubai. router	london. router			mumbai. lan
chennai. router	4	bhopal. router	mumbai. router	colombo. router				chennai. lan
delhi. router	5	colombo. router	bhopal. router	dubai. router	london. router			delhi. lan
colombo. router	3	delhi. router	chennai. router					colombo. lan
dubai. router	4	mumbai. router	delhi. router	london. router				dubai. lan
london. router	7	dubai. router	mumbai. router	delhi. router	boston. router	chicago. router	newyork. router	london. lan
newyork. router	4	london. router	chicago. router	boston. router				newyork. lan
boston. router	5	london. router	newyork. router	chicago. router	seattle. router			boston. lan
chicago. router	5	london. router	newyork. router	boston. router	seattle. router			chicago. lan
seattle. router	3	boston. router	chicago. router					seattle. lan

Airline Flight Routes

Let's make this process less cluttered, as well as more appealing. We'll start by removing the "router" suffixes. And next, let's view these connections as the available flights of an airline on a particular day.

Table 19-2 shows that a few flights have no bookings available, which explains the lack of flights on popular routes like Mumbai to Delhi. (Unfortunately, those good old days when stowaways could make it past security to find accommodation in cargo or Business Class are long past.)

Table 19-2. *Plan of Airline Flight Routes (LS database)*

Originating Airport	no. of links	Destination	Destination	Destination	Destination	Destination	Destination
bhopal	3	chennai	mumbai	delhi			
mumbai	4	chennai	bhopal	dubai	london		
chennai	3	bhopal	mumbai	colombo			
delhi	4	colombo	bhopal	dubai	london		
colombo	2	delhi	chennai				
dubai	3	mumbai	delhi	london			
london	6	dubai	mumbai	delhi	boston	chicago	newyork
newyork	3	london	chicago	boston			
boston	4	london	newyork	chicago	seattle		
chicago	4	london	newyork	boston	seattle		
seattle	2	boston	chicago				

I've also taken the liberty of removing the column of stub LANs. This has been done to declutter the table further, but only for this example. (Ordinarily I would have retained that column as "cities." The stub LANS, or "cities," are connected only to each of the routers (or airports, so to speak). So, if we determine the most appropriate routes to the routers (airports), we will automatically know the routes to those stub LANs (cities).

■ **Note**   There is one point to keep in mind. As per convention, cost is typically associated with the outgoing interface of a router. By that token, the last hop from the final (destination) router to the stub LAN (destination LAN) gets counted as unit cost—that is, if the unit cost per hop is the norm.

What kind of "best flight" options (in terms of minimum number of hops) would a travel agent at Bhopal offer his customers for their destinations from Bhopal? How would he determine that?

We have covered something similar in Chapter 13 (and partly, prior to that, in Chapter 2). The most appropriate routes to various destinations from a particular point are calculated from the overall route plan, or "topology map," as a series of hops or outgoing concentric circles. The traveler starts with destinations[1st degree] and identifies those destinations[1st degree] that become destinations[2nd degree]. The traveler continues this until all the destination options get exhausted.

In our earlier chapter, the Toothpick prepared his own routing table (now presented as Table 19-3). It's obvious that this is not necessarily the only accurate one. Considering the hub at London with flights converging from Mumbai and Delhi, he could have prepared a flight routing table with flights from Bhopal to Delhi, and then onward to London, instead of using Mumbai as the transit point.

Table 19-3. *Toothpick's Flight Plan from Bhopal to All Destinations (Best Routes): Bhopal Airport's Routing Table*

Originating Airport	Degree. of Connections	Destination	Destination	Destination	Destination	Destination	Destination
bhopal	1st degree	chennai	mumbai				delhi
	2nd degree	colombo (via chennai)	dubai (via mumbai)	london (via mumbai)			
	3rd degree			chicago (via london)	boston (via london)	new york (via london)	
	4th degree				seattle (via boston)		

In these kinds of cases, some travelers would prefer the Delhi route while others would prefer the Mumbai route, with other determining factors resulting in reasonable traffic distribution, we hope! And so it is in routing messages as well. Table 19-4 shows an alternate notation.

Table 19-4. *Bhopal Airport's Routing Table (Alternate Notation)*

Originating Airport	Degree. of Connections	Destination Route	Destination Route	Destination Route	Destination Route	Destination Route	Destination Route
bhopal	1st degree	bhopal-chennai	bhopal-mumbai				bhopal-delhi
	2nd degree	bhopal-chennai-colombo	bhopal-mumbai-dubai	bhopal-mumbai-london			
	3rd degree			bhopal-mumbai-london-chicago	bhopal-mumbai-london-boston	bhopal-mumbai-london-new york	
	4th degree				bhopal-mumbai-london-boston-seattle		

Flight Costs and Other Factors

"Ha," I hear you chortle. "Let's be practical. Nobody naively decides a flight route based on just the number of flight hops. There are other pressing factors that are taken into account, such as ticket costs, timing, loyalty points, stopovers, facilities at connecting airports, and so on."

You're absolutely right! We have been considering the most elementary example of "the most appropriate route" calculation until now. And we've done that by assigning only a "unit cost" to each link or hop (connecting flight). That's what's been making the task of calculating the "best routes" to all destinations from a given starting point instinctively easy.

However, things admittedly become more complicated if all the connecting flights in the given example were given different costs (instead of equal preference, or unit cost).

How would you determine the best routes to all the destinations in such a case? How would you do it in comparatively the most efficient manner? Check out Figure 19-2.

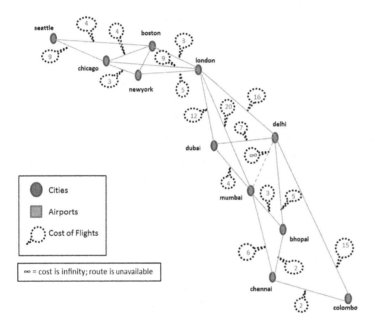

Figure 19-2. *A network of airports connected by flights*

CHAPTER 20

■ ■ ■

Dijkstra's Algorithm — The First Look

> We consider n points (nodes), some or all pairs of which are connected by a branch; the length of each branch is given. We restrict ourselves to the case where at least one path exists between any two nodes.

—E. W. Dijsktra

I'll start the chapter with the description of Dijkstra's algorithm from the Math Wiki site; it's a very elegant description and one that is worth reading[1]:

DIJKSTRA'S ALGORITHM

Dijkstra's algorithm is one of the most widely used methods for finding single-source shortest paths in a simple digraph. In other words, Dijkstra's algorithm determines the shortest paths from a common vertex S to all other vertices in a digraph, if they exist.

Algorithm

Let $G = (V, A)$ be a simple digraph with a function $w(a): A \to \mathbb{R}^+$ which assigns a weight, a non-negative real number, to each arc in G. Fix a source vertex s in G, from which shortest paths will be found.

Additionally, for the purposes of the search itself let $d(v)$ denote the length of the shortest path from s to v. Let S denote the set of visited vertices, i.e., those vertices that have already been examined by the algorithm. Given a path π in G determined by the algorithm, let $p(v)$ denote the predecessor of v for any v in π such that $v \neq s$. The meanings of these additions will become clear in the description of the algorithm. The execution proceeds as follows.

Initial Stage

Let $d(s)=0$. (Since there is no effort in staying in place.)

For each vertex v adjacent from s, let $d(v)$ be $\omega((s,v))$, and let $p(v) = s$.

---

[1]See Math Wiki, http://math.wikia.com/wiki/Dijkstra's_algorithm

For each vertex v such that $v \neq s$ and v is not adjacent from s, let $d(v) = \infty$. (That is, the distance is unknown and v is assumed to be unreachable until it is proven otherwise.)

Let $S = \{s\}$. (Since no paths from s to itself need to be considered.)

Iterative Stage

Determine the vertex v that minimizes $d(v)$ in $V \backslash S$, i.e., an unvisited vertex.

For each vertex u adjacent from v, compare the current value $d(u)$ and $n = d(v) + \omega((v, u))$. If n is the least of the two, let $d(u) = n$, and let $p(u) = v$.

Mark v as visited. That is, let $S = S \cup \{v\}$.

If $S = V$, all vertices have been visited; halt. Otherwise, return to the first step.

Interpretation of Results

When the execution terminates, every vertex v for which $d(v) < \infty$ has a shortest path. This shortest path is determined by repeated application of $p(v)$ to v. For instance, a shortest path from s to v, four vertices long, would be described $(s, p(p(v)), p(v), v)$. For any vertex v where $d(v) = \infty$, there is, of course, no shortest path from s to v.

Because Dijkstra's algorithm is a special case of uniform cost search, where there is no particular goal state, it is essential that $\omega(a) \geq 0$ for all arcs in G.

Puzzles and Algorithms

If you haven't yet aborted your reading, as I did when I first glanced at a similar representation of Dijkstra's algorithm, then you possess deep reserves of courage. The above is just one of many standard, ferocious-looking representations of Dijkstra's algorithm and similar others. When I first looked at one of these I was much younger and more demanding of life. I just knocked the book off the desk in alarm and frustration. For a long while after that, I could not make out the difference between an algorithm and a computer program. Or make my way through either of them.

I must add that there is no error in such representation. It's just that the minimalist style of mathematical representations as explanatory introductions to algorithms are better suited to savants—those who possess gray matter my head doesn't contain. Instead, let's look at algorithms in a different way.

Chapter 19 presented Figure 19-2, which was an example of flight routes and airports to illustrate some points. Let's recast that diagram as Figure 20-1, along with the same assumptions as were made in Chapter 19.

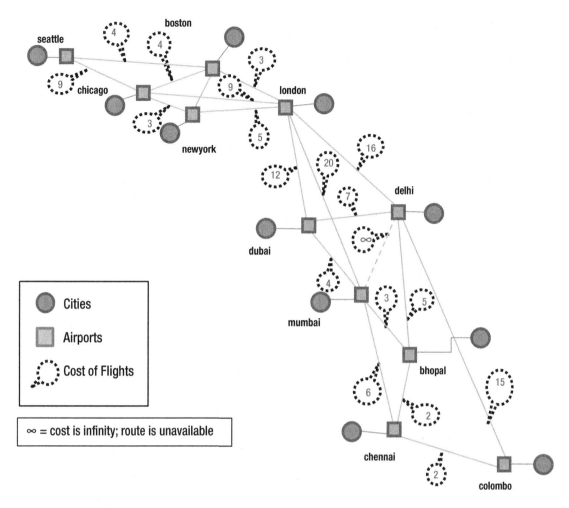

Figure 20-1. *Airports, cities and connecting flights*

If you remember from Chapter 19, the squares are airports, the circles are cities, and the dotted circles show costs of the flights. Think of this as a puzzle. The challenge is to find, in as few steps as possible, a procedure for determining the most appropriate (best) or the lowest-cost paths to all the listed destinations. In our example, there are 10 destination airports apart from Bhopal airport, which is the starting point.

Selecting Specific Members

Unless you is able to solve this airport puzzle immediately, let us digress a bit. In most "selection" problems, the criteria are specific; for example: "From the available group of 10 guys, select those who are 5 feet 9 inches."

The selection criterion in this instance gives a specific, "absolute" way for making immediate comparisons while you're considering the various members of the sample set. So the procedure for solving the problem in the minimum number of steps is quite simple and should be something along these lines:

Algorithm A

1. Let the heights of the respective persons be:

   H(0), H(1), H(2), H(3), H(4), H(5), H(6), H(7), H(8), H(9)

2. Let the random list of the heights of the 10 concerned persons be called Group.

3. Create an empty list called Queue to store the heights of those persons equal to 5 feet 9inches.

4. If H(0) = 5ft9″, save in Queue, else ignore.

5. If H(1) = 5ft9″, save in Queue, else ignore.

6. If H(2) = 5ft9″, save in Queue, else ignore.

7. Repeat for next 6 members.

8. If H(9) = 5ft9″, save in Queue, else ignore.

9. End.

Arranging Members in Order of Height

Let's give a different spin to the problem. Let the problem statement now be: "Arrange the persons in the group in order of height, starting from the shortest and going to the tallest."

Unlike the previous problem, this has not provided an "absolute" selection criterion. Instead, it has given a "comparative" criterion. The problem is that such a comparative criterion keeps changing. That makes it necessary for us to keep recalibrating the measure in our mind while we consider almost every member of the set.

So, how do we tackle such a problem? My instinctive approach would be to:

Algorithm B

1. Let the heights of the respective persons be:

   H(0), H(1), H(2), H(3), H(4), H(5), H(6), H(7), H(8), H(9)

2. Let the random list of the heights of the 10 concerned persons be called Group.

3. Create an empty list called Queue to store the heights of the same persons in increasing order.

4. Let the first element/slot of Queue, Q(1), be used to store the height of the shortest person.

5. If H(0) < H(1), save H(0) in Q(1), Else save H(1) in Q(1).

6. If H(2) < Q(1), save in Q(1), else ignore.

▒ **Note**   For Q(1), the reference is to the current content of Q(1), which could be either H(0) or H(1). If H(2) is shorter than the current content, it will be written over the other.

---

    7.   If H(3) < Q(1), save in Q(1), else ignore.

▒ **Note**   For Q(1), the reference is to the current content of Q(1), which could be H(0) or H(1) or H(2). If H(3) is shorter than the current content, it will be written over the other.

---

    8.   Repeat for next 5 members.

    9.   If H(9) < Q(1), save in Q(1), else ignore.

▒ **Note**   For Q(1), the reference is to the current content of Q(1), which could any of the heights from H(0) to H(8). If H(9) is shorter than the current content, it will be written over the other.

---

    10.   End.

We have to keep in mind that solving the problem is actually no great challenge. The real challenge lies in completing it efficiently (e.g., in as few steps as possible, without error). We are referring to comparative improvements here.

From that perspective, this answer would probably be labeled in expert circles as the "slash-and-burn approach." By the time we were to reach instruction 4, the experts would have slashed their own wrists, so great would be the injury to their superior algorithmic sensibilities.

To be fair, fulfilment of the designated requirement as well as improvements in the solution would depend on the system's design parameters—the resources that the system has, such as the amount of working memory (scratch pad), memory addresses, available instructions, and so on. In other words, we need information about available or possible resources and system capabilities to create an optimal solution to a problem.

▒ **Note**   I have left Algorithm B incomplete to prove a point. This is actually a decent puzzle to consider the various possible solutions, along with their trade-offs. I identified the shortest person in the group. How about the other nine persons in order of height?

Many of these wide-search algorithmic challenges are tackled by narrowing the field—that is, if categorical selection criteria are not available, you look for qualifying criteria to create smaller groups so as to narrow the search. Any such approach is an improvement, if even it's to just start the search!

When you use two different-purpose criteria or use a series of such criteria—qualifiers leading to selectors—the procedure is akin to using a series of ever-smaller sieves to sift through sand. Such an analogy is poignant for me, as it reminds me of happier childhood days when my brother played with such sieves and pans in the sand. However, the sieve analogy is not new to mathematics nor to computer science; it's been used for a long time in regard to prime numbers.

The Shortest Airplane Route

Let's return now to the airports and flight plan puzzle presented earlier: "find the lowest-cost route."
A passenger typically looks for the best route to a given single destination, based on certain criteria in his mind. The most important of these criteria likely is flight cost, but it could also be availability or even shortness of route. So let's assume that the passenger accords weight to each of the parameters that he considers are important in his selection of route.

Apart from a few direct-flight links, it is reasonable to expect most routes consist of multiple constituent links, or hops. There is the reality of a finite number of flights each day. But apart from that, multiple flight preferences can cause differing variations in route identification; it is possible, if not reasonable, to expect flight routes to consist of more than one constituent link or hop (i.e., even for those destinations that have direct flights). So the passenger needs a procedure (sequence of steps)—an algorithm—that determines the best route from the many available alternatives.

Some Considerations

Things would be quite simple, of course, if all the routes consisted of single hops (links). Unfortunately, they do not; this is one of the main causes of the "greedy" nature of the algorithm design—its insistence on determining the shortest paths to *all* the listed destinations (as opposed to just evaluating some of the available paths to one destination). The design objective, then, is categorical: the most appropriate path to the destination needs to be selected.

Let's continue to assume that the most appropriate route for a particular passenger is the lowest-cost route to his destination. The route/path to his destination traverses multiple links in a complex flight chart that has numerous intersections. So how do we commence determining the shortest route to this identified destination? I think no one will refute the logic of the following reasoning:

1. Route to destination = intermediate (route 1 + route 2 + …)

2. Shortest route to destination = shortest intermediate (route 1 + route 2 + …)

3. Hence: Equation A: Shortest route to destination = shortest intermediate route 1 + shortest intermediate route 2 + …

■ **Note**   The iterative nature of the search is the other chief characteristic of the "greedy" algorithm.

In case there are readers wondering whether such mathematical properties can happily be transposed across brackets without penalty, know that you're a gifted (questioning) mathematician waiting to be discovered. For those who are satisfied with the assurance of the thumb's rule, surely you can't expect the shortest route to have a constituent route that is any longer than needed. Or, can you?

The point is that if we are insisting the route to that destination be the shortest possible, we have to concede that the shortest route will consist of intermediate routes that are themselves the shortest possible routes.

To illustrate the point, let the shortest or lowest-cost route from A to B, with A as the source and B as the destination, be AB:

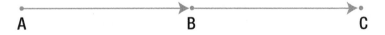

A   B   C

If the shortest or lowest-cost route from B to C, with B as the origin and C as the destination, is BC, then the shortest or lowest-cost route from A to C, with A as origin and C as destination, will necessarily be (AB + BC).

Thus, any procedure or solution for determining the best or most appropriate route to a destination has to proceed on the assumption that it will consist of a combination of intermediate best routes.

Also, these intermediate best routes cannot be guessed in advance. All possibilities need to be systematically considered, which invariably results in the calculation of best routes to other destinations for purposes of consideration or elimination—even if later some of these routes are found to be unnecessary or undesired, and hence are discarded. This conclusion will become more evident when we see Dijkstra's algorithm in operation in the next chapter.

CHAPTER 21

■ ■ ■

Dijkstra's Algorithm – The Closest Look

Whenever there is a hard job to be done I assign it to a lazy man; he is sure to find an easy way of doing it.

—Walter Chrysler

Chapter 20 introduced Dijkstra's algorithm. Here, we take a closer look at its workings, picking up the example we've been using of the airline flight plan. We use the algorithm to first determine the shortest among the links directly connected to the origin, so as to find the destination closest to it. Then we determine the shortest of the remaining links, as well as those directly connected to the previously identified closest destination, thereby finding the next closest destination. This process is continued until all the destinations and links are identified. It a process that makes solving the puzzle easier and faster.

But first, here's the best description of Dijkstra's algorithm:

Dijkstra's algorithm is a simple algorithm that efficiently calculates all at once the shortest paths to all destinations. The algorithm incrementally calculates a tree of shortest paths. It begins with the calculating router adding itself to the tree. All of the router's neighbors are then added to a candidate list, with costs equal to the cost of the links from the router to the neighbors. The router on the candidate list with the smallest cost is then added to the shortest-path tree, and that router's neighbors are then examined for inclusion in (or modification of) the candidate list. The algorithm then iterates until the candidate list is empty.

—John Moy, *OSPF-Anatomy of a Routing Protocol*, Section 4.8

Now, let's look at how this algorithm is applied to our ongoing example and thus how it applies to the network domain.

The Puzzle of Finding the Cheapest Flight

For the organizational network, when the link between each router and its neighbor has a cost associated with it, the cost gets noted as an entry in an important field in the Link State Advertisement (LSA), called the *metric field*. Cost is a property (an arbitrary number) associated with the link connecting neighboring routers. It gets noted as many times in the LSA as there are active neighbors to the router.

As stated in earlier chapters, we are concerned with a network of routers, stub LANs and links that, in our ongoing puzzle, we have been viewing as a network of airports, cities, and connecting flights. We are, for this example, ignoring the cities (stub LANs); see Chapter 19 for our justification in this particular case.

Figure 21-1 shows the flight network we have been using to illustrate the network domain. The figure shows the cost metrics much as it would appear in a representation of the converged (identical) Link State databases of the network's routers.

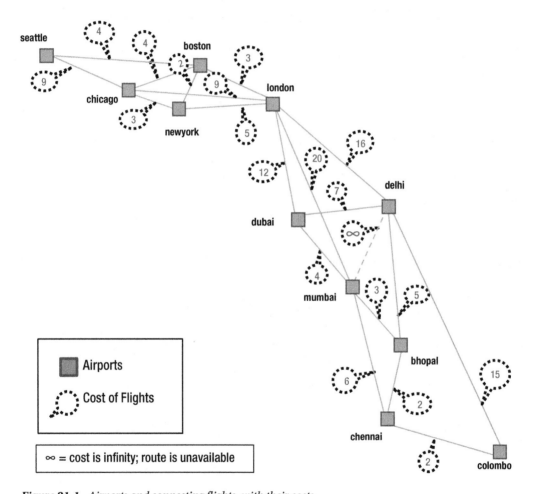

Figure 21-1. *Airports and connecting flights, with their costs*

Table 21-1 similarly shows the destinations[1st degree] and their associated costs. Note that the cost associated with any destination in a cell corresponds to the cost of the link connecting the originating airport with the destination airport (in either direction).

Table 21-1. Overall Flight Route Table (LSDB) Showing Destinations|1st Degree

Originating Airport	no. of links	Destination	Destination	Destination	Destination	Destination	Destination
bhopal	3	chennai cost=2	mumbai cost=3	delhi cost=5			
mumbai	4	chennai cost=6	bhopal cost=3	dubai cost=4	london cost=20		
chennai	3	bhopal cost=2	mumbai cost=6	colombo cost=2			
delhi	4	colombo cost=1	bhopal cost=5	dubai cost=7	london cost=16		
colombo	2	delhi cost=1	chennai cost=2				
dubai	3	mumbai cost=4	delhi cost=7	london cost=12			
london	6	dubai cost=12	mumbai cost=20	delhi cost=16	boston cost=3	chicago cost=9	newyork cost=5
newyork	3	london cost=5	chicago cost=3	boston cost=2			
boston	4	london cost=3	newyork cost=2	chicago cost=4	seattle cost=4		
chicago	4	london cost=9	newyork cost=3	boston cost=4	seattle cost=9		
seattle	2	boston cost=4	chicago cost=9				

■ **Note**   As a configuration item, cost is typically assigned to the outgoing interface of a router. So, if it is said that a link has a single associated cost, it has to be the result of assigning the connecting interfaces a common cost at the opposite ends. In such a case, travel along the link in either direction incurs the same cost.

Now, let us start working on Table 21-1.

Note in Table 21-1 that Chennai (cost = 2), Mumbai (cost = 3), and Delhi (cost = 5) are destinations|1st degree for Bhopal airport. However, there is no guarantee that the three cities are necessarily closer (lower in cost) to Bhopal than might be any other airport, despite only three of them being directly connected to Bhopal. For example, consider Colombo, which is connected to Chennai with an associated cost of 2. Chennai is directly connected to Bhopal, also with an associated cost of 2. The total travel cost from Bhopal to Colombo, then, is 4, which is lower than that between Bhopal and Delhi.

Considering the Indirect Route

The lowest-cost route from origin to destination need not always be the most direct route or the direct link between the two points. For example, in Figure 21-2, the shortest distance between A and C is not the route AC, but the route AB + BC.

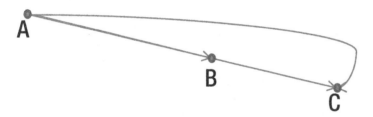

Figure 21-2. *Direct routes are not necessarily the shortest routes*

In Figure 21-3, the distance to C1 from O is the same as the distance to B1 from O, because C1 and B1 have the same degree of separation from the origin, O.

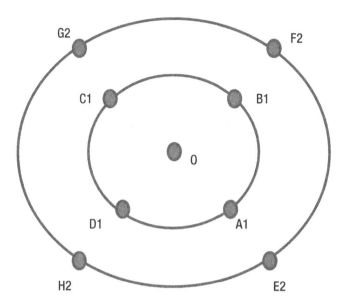

Figure 21-3. *Arrangement of destinations in equidistant concentric circles around the origin*

In Figure 21-3, the distance to G2 from O is the same as the distance to E2 from O. This equality occurs when the weight (distance/cost) assigned to every hop to various destinations is the same.

■ **Note** The weight (distance/cost) associated with each hop between sites may vary, resulting in different distances from the origin to destinations of the same degree of separation, reflected in the irregular circles around the origin, shown in Figure 21-4.

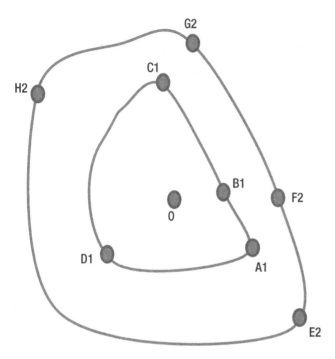

Figure 21-4. *Arrangement of destinations around the origin, based on their degree of separation from the origin*

In Figure 21-4, the distance to F2 from O, via B1, is probably less than the distance to C1 from O, though C1 is directly connected to the origin while F2 is separated from origin O by two degrees.

The absence of a consistent selection criterion for choosing the required route is what complicated this puzzle at the start. But we now have a comparative selection criterion—the path with the lowest cost. As indicated in the earlier chapter, one way to make our task easier is to find other *qualifying criteria* so that the search is faster.

Remember that no destination gets "eliminated." The destinations are just arranged in a queue in order of their cost relative to Bhopal Airport. So when we refer to "qualifying criteria," these are properties that make the natural ordering of these destinations easier or faster. The purpose of any network filtering or sorting method is the same. It is not elimination but, rather, a useful ordering of the elements. It is the qualifying properties that justify the arrangement of candidates in the queue.

The Algorithmic Approach

Now, how do we go about this network finding the most appropriate (lowest-cost) routes to all the destinations from Bhopal, using a methodical, algorithmically described manner. This is preferable to the slash-and-burn approach employed earlier in this book.

So, let's explore some of these more efficient alternatives by moving some of those destinations into an advance group that's based on some qualifying criterion. That way, instead of making comparisons within a common large group, which takes the greater effort, we narrow the search by creating a smaller group.

Here are some obvious guidelines we can begin using:

1. The destination closest to the origin will be one from among all the directly connected locations. (No route to such a destination can bypass *all* the directly connected locations.)

2. The next closest destination will then be from among the previous candidates (since any other routes will have to pass through them) or those directly connected to the recently determined closest destination (for the same reason). The list of candidates thus has been widened by this iteration.

3. The procedure is repeated.

So, now we have two groups:

- The locations that are either directly connected to the origin or that are directly connected to the recently declared/determined closest destinations.

- The declared closest destinations.

Now, let us mechanize the above thoughts. There is a general set or group of locations, one of which is later identified as the origin. For the sake of mathematical neatness, the same location is typically treated as the double of the origin; a twin entity. Hence the distance between the origin and itself is considered to be zero, whenever that corresponding variable appears in an equation. First, we define those two lists:

- List A (also called "candidate list") consists of locations that are directly connected to the origin or other locations in List B.

- List B is locations closest to the origin, whose shortest or lowest-cost route has been determined. This has been determined from among the available locations in List A, the candidate list.

Here is the logic behind having two such lists:

- One list (List B) is the list of destinations whose routes from the origin have already been determined to be the shortest.

- The candidate list (List A) has locations whose routes will necessarily have to pass through already existing/determined shortest routes.

So, the basic principle of Dijkstra's algorithm is pretty simple: Determine the first few of the direct links from the origin that are the shortest (in the right order); the subsequent shortest routes will necessarily be links belonging to the first set.

The Procedure

As a kid, I remember my brother used to have an array of sieves to play with. Let's use two of those sieves to help us understand this exercise.

- *Sieve 1* filters through or selects only those locations (candidates) from the general group that are either directly connected to the origin or are directly connected to other locations in List B. This is List A, the candidate list.

- *Sieve 2* filters through or selects the location closest to the origin. This is selected from among the available locations in List A, the candidate list.

Here's the process:

1. We have n = 10 unique locations in the general group to start.

2. Pass n unique locations through Sieve 1.

3. Save output in List A.

4. If duplicate (origin-to-destination) pairs appear, remove those with higher route costs.

5. Pass candidate list through Sieve 2.

6. Save lowest-cost destination in List B.

7. Until n = 0, A = 0, repeat statement 2 to statement 6.

8. Then end.

Let's apply the programming process to Table 21-4.

Table 21-4. Overall Flight Route Table (LSDB) Showing Destinations and Connecting Flight with Lowest Associated Costs

Originating Airport	no. of links	Destination	Destination	Destination	Destination	Destination	Destination
bhopal's 1st Degree Destinations	3	chennai cost=2	mumbai cost=3			delhi cost=5	
2nd Degree Destinations		colombo cost=4 via chennai	dubai cost=7 via mumbai				
3rd Degree Destinations			london cost=19 via dubai				
4th Degree Destinations			chicago cost=28 via london	boston cost=22 via london	newyork cost=24 via london		
5th Degree Destinations				seattle cost=26 via boston			
mumbai	4	chennai cost=6	bhopal cost=3	dubai cost=4	london cost=20		
chennai	3	bhopal cost=2	mumbai cost=6	colombo cost=2			
delhi	4	colombo cost=1	bhopal cost=5	dubai cost=7	london cost=16		

(continued)

Table 21-4. (*continued*)

Originating Airport	no. of links	Destination	Destination	Destination	Destination	Destination	Destination
colombo	2	delhi cost=1	chennai cost=2				
dubai	3	mumbai cost=4	delhi cost=7	london cost=12			
london	6	dubai cost=12	mumbai cost=20	delhi cost=16	boston cost=3	chicago cost=9	newyork cost=5
newyork	3	london cost=5	chicago cost=3	boston cost=2			
boston	4	london cost=3	newyork cost=2	chicago cost=4	seattle cost=4		
chicago	4	london cost=9	newyork cost=3	boston cost=4	seattle cost=9		
Seattle	2	boston cost=4	chicago cost=9				

Did your calculations turn out like this? A little bit of practice helps to make the scribbling a bit more legible and sensible! If you notice, I prefer to make a note of the prior transit airport at the bottom of the cell. It helps keep me honest.

The same exercise is shown pictorially, step by step, in Figures 21-5 through 21-15. *Happy OSPF!*

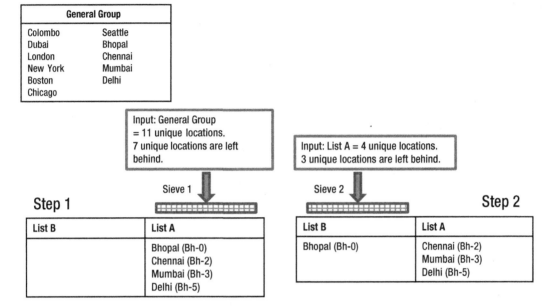

Figure 21-5. First sift with sieves 1 and 2

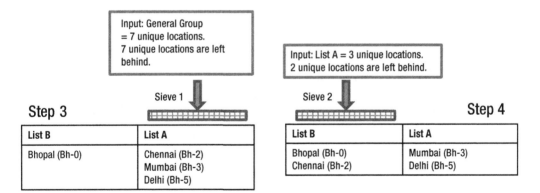

Figure 21-6. Second sift with sieves 1 and 2

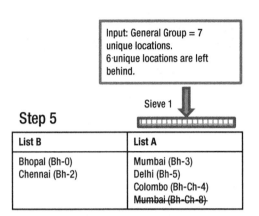

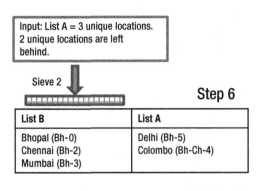

Step 5

List B	List A
Bhopal (Bh-0) Chennai (Bh-2)	Mumbai (Bh-3) Delhi (Bh-5) Colombo (Bh-Ch-4) ~~Mumbai (Bh-Ch-8)~~

Step 6

List B	List A
Bhopal (Bh-0) Chennai (Bh-2) Mumbai (Bh-3)	Delhi (Bh-5) Colombo (Bh-Ch-4)

Figure 21-7. *Third sift with sieves 1 and 2*

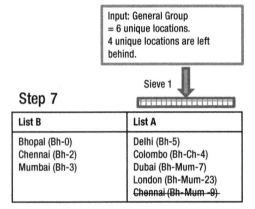

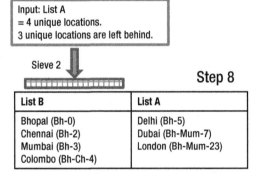

Step 7

List B	List A
Bhopal (Bh-0) Chennai (Bh-2) Mumbai (Bh-3)	Delhi (Bh-5) Colombo (Bh-Ch-4) Dubai (Bh-Mum-7) London (Bh-Mum-23) ~~Chennai (Bh-Mum-9)~~

Step 8

List B	List A
Bhopal (Bh-0) Chennai (Bh-2) Mumbai (Bh-3) Colombo (Bh-Ch-4)	Delhi (Bh-5) Dubai (Bh-Mum-7) London (Bh-Mum-23)

Figure 21-8. *Fourth sift with sieves 1 and 2*

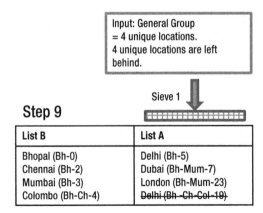

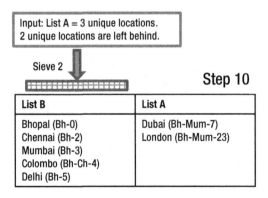

Step 9

List B	List A
Bhopal (Bh-0) Chennai (Bh-2) Mumbai (Bh-3) Colombo (Bh-Ch-4)	Delhi (Bh-5) Dubai (Bh-Mum-7) London (Bh-Mum-23) ~~Delhi (Bh-Ch-Col-19)~~

Step 10

List B	List A
Bhopal (Bh-0) Chennai (Bh-2) Mumbai (Bh-3) Colombo (Bh-Ch-4) Delhi (Bh-5)	Dubai (Bh-Mum-7) London (Bh-Mum-23)

Figure 21-9. *Fifth sift with sieves 1 and 2*

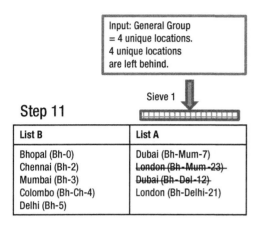

Input: General Group
= 4 unique locations.
4 unique locations
are left behind.

Input: List A = 2 unique locations.
1 unique locations are left behind.

Sieve 1

Sieve 2

Step 11

Step 12

List B	List A
Bhopal (Bh-0)	Dubai (Bh-Mum-7)
Chennai (Bh-2)	~~London (Bh-Mum-23)~~
Mumbai (Bh-3)	~~Dubai (Bh-Del-12)~~
Colombo (Bh-Ch-4)	London (Bh-Delhi-21)
Delhi (Bh-5)	

List B	List A
Bhopal (Bh-0)	London (Bh-Mum-23)
Chennai (Bh-2)	
Mumbai (Bh-3)	
Colombo (Bh-Ch-4)	
Delhi (Bh-5)	
Dubai (Bh-Mum-7)	

Figure 21-10. *Sixth sift with sieves 1 and 2*

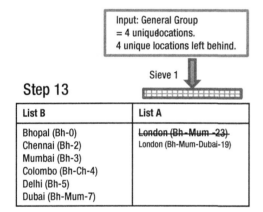

Input: General Group
= 4 unique locations.
4 unique locations left behind.

Input: List A = 1 unique location.
0 unique locations are left behind.

Sieve 1

Sieve 2

Step 13

Step 14

List B	List A
Bhopal (Bh-0)	~~London (Bh-Mum-23)~~
Chennai (Bh-2)	London (Bh-Mum-Dubai-19)
Mumbai (Bh-3)	
Colombo (Bh-Ch-4)	
Delhi (Bh-5)	
Dubai (Bh-Mum-7)	

List B	List A
Bhopal (Bh-0)	
Chennai (Bh-2)	
Mumbai (Bh-3)	
Colombo (Bh-Ch-4)	
Delhi (Bh-5)	
Dubai (Bh-Mum-7)	
London (Bh-Mum-Dubai-19)	

Figure 21-11. *Seventh sift with sieves 1 and 2*

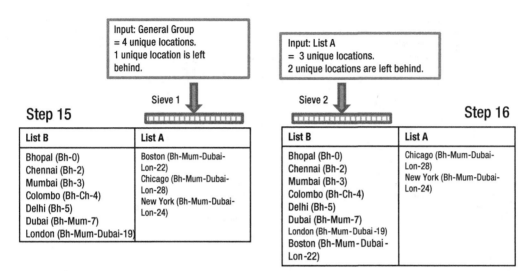

Figure 21-12. *Eighth sift with sieves 1 and 2*

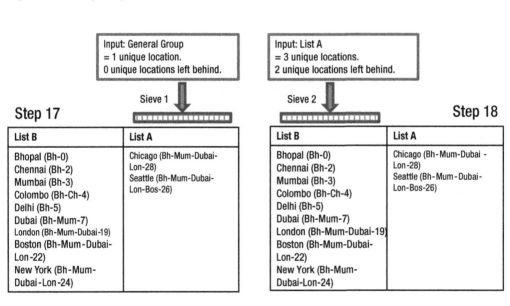

Figure 21-13. *Ninth sift with sieves 1 and 2*

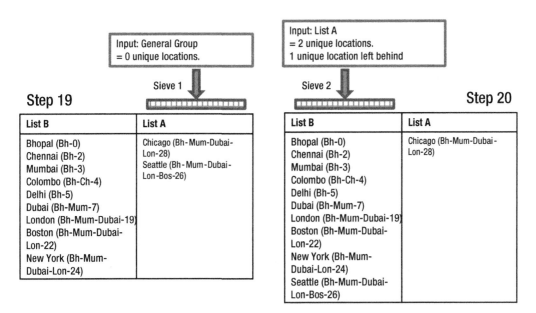

Figure 21-14. *Tenth sift with sieves 1 and 2*

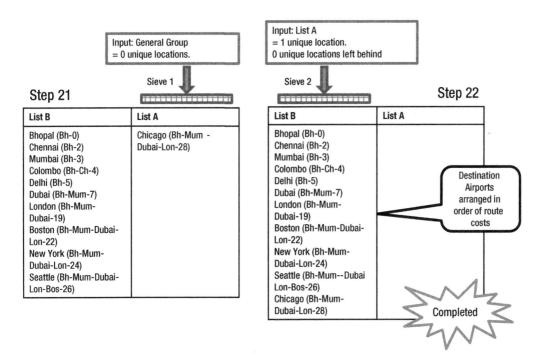

Figure 21-15. *Eleventh sift with sieves 1 and 2*

Every problem becomes very childish when once it is explained to you.
—Arthur Conan Doyle, *Sherlock Holmes, the Adventure of the Dancing Men*

CHAPTER 22

Bibliography

No matter what anybody tells you, words and ideas can change the world.

—Robin Williams as John Keating, in the movie *Dead Poets Society*

Published References

Comer, Douglas. *Internetworking with TCP/IP*, Vol. 1, 6th Ed. Saddle River, NJ: Pearson, 2013.
Doyle, Jeff. *Routing TCP IP*, Vol. 1. Indianapolis: Cisco Press, 1998.
Kozierok, Charles. *The TCP IP Guide: A Comprehensive, Illustrated Internet Protocols Reference.* San Francisco: No Starch Press, 2005.
Medhi, Deepankar. *Network Routing: Algorithms, Protocols, and Architectures.* San Francisco: Morgan Kaufmann Publishers, 2007.
Moy, John. *OSPF: Anatomy of a Routing Protocol.* Boston: Addison-Wesley Professional, 1998.
Osterlow, Heather. *IP Routing Primer Plus.* Indianapolis: Sams Publishing, 2012.
Puzmanova, Rita. *Routing and Switching: Time of Convergence.* Boston: Addison-Wesley Professional, 1998.

Internet References

RFC2328: OSPF Version 2
http://www.rfc-editor.org/rfc/rfc2328.txt
On Dijkstra's algorithm, see
http://en.wikipedia.org/wiki/Dijkstra's_algorithm or
http://en.wikibooks.org/wiki/Artificial_Intelligence/Search/Dijkstra's_Algorithm.
On Dijkstra's algorithm simulation, see
http://optlab-server.sce.carleton.ca/POAnimations2007/DijkstrasAlgo.html (an open-source site).
On Dijkstra's algorithm revisited and the OR/MS connection, see
http://www.ifors.ms.unimelb.edu.au/tutorial/dijkstra_new/.
On the proof of Dijkstra's algorithm, see
https://www.cs.auckland.ac.nz/~jmor159/PLDS210/dij-proof.html/
http://math.wikia.com/wiki/Dijkstra's_algorithm
On graph theory, see
http://en.wikipedia.org/wiki/Graph_theory.
On the traveling salesman problem—nearest neighbor algorithm, see
http://en.wikipedia.org/wiki/Nearest_neighbour_algorithm.

Index

Get the eBook for only $5!

Why limit yourself?

Now you can take the weightless companion with you wherever you go and access your content on your PC, phone, tablet, or reader.

Since you've purchased this print book, we're happy to offer you the eBook in all 3 formats for just $5.

Convenient and fully searchable, the PDF version enables you to easily find and copy code—or perform examples by quickly toggling between instructions and applications. The MOBI format is ideal for your Kindle, while the ePUB can be utilized on a variety of mobile devices.

To learn more, go to www.apress.com/companion or contact support@apress.com.

Apress®
THE EXPERT'S VOICE™

Printed in the United States
By Bookmasters